NorthStar

READING AND WRITING
Intermediate

SECOND EDITION

Laurie Barton
Carolyn Dupaquier Sardinas

Series Editors
Frances Boyd
Carol Numrich

Longman

NorthStar: Reading and Writing, Intermediate, Second Edition
Teacher's Manual and Achievement Tests

Pearson Education, 10 Bank Street, White Plains, NY 10606

Teacher's Manual by Laurie Barton
Achievement Tests by Tay Lesley

Development director: Penny Laporte
Project manager: Debbie Sistino
Development editor: Stacey Hunter
Vice president, director of design and production: Rhea Banker
Executive managing editor: Linda Moser
Production editor: Marc Oliver
Production manager: Liza Pleva
Production coordinator: Melissa Leyva
Director of manufacturing: Patrice Fraccio
Senior manufacturing buyer: Dave Dickey
Cover design: Rhea Banker
Text design: Quorum Creative Services
Text composition: TSI Graphics
Text font: 11/13 Sabon

ISBN 0-201-78842-X

LONGMAN ON THE **WEB**

Longman.com offers online resources for
teachers and students. Access our Companion
Websites, our online catalog, and our local
offices around the world.

Visit us at **longman.com**.

Printed in the United States of America
6 7 8 9 10—TCS—09 08 07 06 05

Contents

Teacher's Manual

Achievement Tests

Introduction to Achievement Tests   107

Achievement Tests

Achievement Tests:
Test 1 Answer Key   109

Introduction to the *NorthStar* Series

The *NorthStar* Approach to Language Teaching   *NorthStar* is a five-level, integrated skills series for language learning. The series is divided into two strands: listening and speaking, and reading and writing. There are five books in each strand, taking students from the high beginning level of the *Introductory Student Book* to the advanced level of the *Advanced Student Book*. At each level, the two strands explore different aspects of the same contemporary themes. Each book practices language-learning skills through high-interest thematic content.

In addition to the Student Books, the *Writing Activity Book* for each level of the reading and writing strand expands and reinforces the writing process. The *Audio Program* includes, on CD or cassette, all the reading and listening segments as well as pronunciation exercises. The *Video Program* includes 3- to 5-minute segments for each unit. The segments are thematically linked to the units in the Student Books to offer additional material for listening comprehension and discussion or writing.

Integrated skills are at the heart of the *NorthStar* series. When two or more language skills are combined, language learning is apt to be more authentic, natural, and motivating. Integrating skills offers more opportunity for recycling and reinforcing key vocabulary, grammatical structures, and ideas. As a result, students have more occasions to assimilate information and language, thereby facilitating learning.

Approach to Reading and Writing   *NorthStar* supports the approach that learning to be a good writer means learning to be a good reader, and vice versa. Reading skills are taught *implicitly* throughout each unit. For example, the comprehension exercises are designed to give practice in reading skills, such as predicting, identifying main ideas and details, skimming and scanning.

Writing skills are taught *implicitly* through the readings: The readings serve as models of good writing. In the Style section, writing skills are taught *explicitly* through analysis, explanation, and guided practice. The writing process begins at the start of each unit (often with the first Prediction exercise), continues through the unit (with dialogues, written reactions to a partner's comments, chart completion, note taking), includes the Style section (with explicit writing skills and structured practice), and culminates in the Writing Topics section, where students are asked to produce a complete piece of writing.

Reading and writing skills—including strategies for improving vocabulary, comprehension, and grammar—are cultivated in every section of every unit. In the Research Topics section, the reading and writing integration becomes most clear and relevant, as students are asked to conduct research and read texts from a variety of authentic sources and then integrate ideas from these sources into their own writing.

Approach to Listening and Speaking   *NorthStar* provides structured opportunities for students to practice listening to many types of discourse. Listening skills are taught *implicitly* throughout each unit. For example, the comprehension exercises are designed to give practice in such listening skills as predicting, identifying main ideas and details, and note taking.

Speaking skills are taught *implicitly* through the listenings: The listenings serve as models of functional language or conventional style. In the Style section, speaking skills are taught *explicitly* though analysis, explanation, a carefully structured pronunciation syllabus, and guided practice. The teaching of speaking begins at the start of each unit (often with the first Prediction exercise), continues through the unit (with categorizing and ranking activities, interviews, games, pronunciation practice, comparing answers and discussing differences, sharing opinions), includes the Style section (with explicit functional skills and structured practice), and culminates in the Speaking Topics section, where students use their speaking skills to create role plays, case studies, debates, radio announcements, and presentations.

Listening and speaking skills—including learning strategies for improving vocabulary, comprehension, and grammar—are cultivated in every section of every unit. In the Research Topics section, the listening and speaking integration becomes most clear and relevant, as students are asked to conduct projects such as surveys or in-person and telephone interviews and then integrate ideas from these sources into their own oral presentations.

Approach to Grammar   Content drives the organization of the grammar syllabus. Accordingly, students have opportunities to encounter and work with grammar structures in authentic contexts. The purpose of the grammar section is to enable clear and accurate discussion and writing about the unit theme.

The Grammar section of each unit is not intended to be an exhaustive treatment of a grammatical point. Rather, it is an opportunity for students to focus on a new or familiar point within the specific context of the unit. Teachers and students can use the Grammar section either as the first step in presenting a particular structure or as a review. For more detailed explanations of the grammar points, a chart of Grammar Book References is included in the Student Books. This chart cross-references the unit grammar to appropriate sections in two successful grammar series: Azar's Grammar series and *Focus on Grammar*.

Grammar is taught both inductively (through discovery) and deductively (through explanation). First, students answer questions to discover the form, usage, and meaning of the grammar. Next, they read an explanation of the point, with examples in the thematic context of the unit. Finally, students practice the structures in exercises related to the content of the unit.

Approach to Vocabulary   Vocabulary practice has been increased in the Second Edition of *NorthStar*. Vocabulary is taught both *directly* and *indirectly*. Specific vocabulary exercises focus on meaning, usage, and word forms. In many of the other exercises (grammar, style, speaking/writing topics, research), the vocabulary reappears but is not the focus of the exercise.

In Section 1, Focus on the Topic, vocabulary has been chosen for its relevance in discussing the topic/theme. In other cases, the vocabulary is essential for comprehension of a listening or reading text, so the focus becomes preteaching vocabulary for comprehension. In Section 3, Focus on Vocabulary, the work takes on a different focus, as words are reviewed and studied in more depth. In this section, students are asked to go beyond the vocabulary presented in the text and explore new items. In the listening and speaking strand, a particular effort has been made to focus on idiomatic and informal expressions that are common in spoken English.

A Message from the Series Editors

We think of a good textbook as a musical score or a movie script. It tells you the moves and roughly how quickly and in what sequence to make them. But until you and your students bring it to life, a book is silent and static, a mere possibility. We hope that *NorthStar* orients, guides, and interests you as teachers.

It is our hope that the *NorthStar* series stimulates your students' thinking, which in turn stimulates their language learning, and that they will have many opportunities to reflect on the viewpoints of journalists, commentators, researchers, other students, and people in the community. Further, we hope that *NorthStar* guides them to develop their own points of view on the many and varied themes encompassed by this series.

We welcome your comments and questions. Please send them to us at the publisher:

Frances Boyd and Carol Numrich, Series Editors
NorthStar
Pearson Education
10 Bank Street
White Plains, NY 10606

Overview of the *Teacher's Manual and Achievement Tests*

The *NorthStar Teacher's Manual and Achievement Tests* includes:

- Specific suggestions for teaching each unit, including:
  - ✓ Unit-by-unit overview (scope and sequence) and summary
  - ✓ Unit-by-unit description of the Focus, Set Up, and Expansion/Homework activities for each exercise
  - ✓ Suggested teaching times
  - ✓ Cross-references to the companion strand, Grammar Book References, *Writing Activity Book,* Video Program, and Companion Website
- The Answer Key to the Student Book
- Reproducible Achievement Tests with Answer Keys—including the test audioscript and test audio CD for the *Listening and Speaking* strand; and a test-generating CD-ROM to allow teachers to customize and adapt the 300 test items and writing tasks on the Reading and Writing Achievement Tests for the *Reading and Writing* strand
- An alphabetized-by-unit word list of the key vocabulary items practiced in each unit

COURSE PLANNER

Each unit contains approximately eight hours of classroom material, plus expansion, homework, and support material. Teachers can customize the units by assigning some exercises for homework and/or eliminating others. To help teachers customize the units for their specific teaching situation, the Unit-by-Unit Teaching Suggestions in the *Teacher's Manual* include 1, 2, or 3 stars to indicate the relative importance of each section or exercise:

> ✪✪✪ **Essential** sections
> ✪✪ **Recommended** sections
> ✪ **Optional** sections

To use *NorthStar* most effectively, see the teaching guide below.

CLASS TIME AVAILABLE PER UNIT	SECTIONS TO COMPLETE
8 hours or more	Essential (✪✪✪), Recommended (✪✪), Optional (✪)
6 hours	Essential (✪✪✪), Recommended (✪✪)
4 hours	Essential (✪✪✪) only

The World of Advertising

OVERVIEW

Theme:	Advertising

Readings:	*Advertising All Over the World*
	    A magazine article
	Changing World Markets
	    An excerpt from a speech

Critical Thinking Skills:	Compare personal buying habits Identify and later reevaluate assumptions Infer information not explicit in the texts Connect themes between texts Compare and contrast advertising compaigns
Reading Tasks:	Make predictions Identify main ideas Read for details Support answers with evidence from the texts Relate information in the text to life experience Research local advertising campaigns
Writing Tasks:	Write a paragraph with a topic sentence, supporting details, and a concluding sentence Write a letter in response to a speech Write a commercial Describe a product Compile data with a graphic organizer
Vocabulary:	Word definitions Context clues Synonyms Idioms
Grammar:	Contrast simple present and present progressive

UNIT SUMMARY

This unit deals with the legal, linguistic, and cultural challenges faced by global advertisers. Reading One is an article on global advertising. Reading Two is the transcript of a speech on the changing markets in Russia and China.

The companion unit in *NorthStar: Listening and Speaking* deals with advertising on the air.

1 Focus on the Topic, PAGE 1

✪✪✪ A   PREDICTING

Suggested Time: 10 minutes 🕐

Focus
To get students thinking about various aspects of advertising: product, market, and media.

Setup
Ask the students to identify the product in the picture. Ask if they have seen similar ads for this product. Discuss Exercises 1 and 2, encouraging them to give detailed answers.

Expansion/Homework
Have students work in pairs to answer question 2 by writing a brief advertising message. Give them the following model: *Drink powerful Pepsi for a cool taste. It's refreshing!* Encourage them to think of other words that describe the product. Then ask them to read their advertisements aloud.

Link to *NorthStar: Listening and Speaking*
Ask students to consider what kind of sound effects could be used in advertising this product on the radio.

✪✪ B   SHARING INFORMATION

Suggested Time: 20 minutes 🕐

Focus
To get students thinking more specifically about the real products they buy and the ways in which these products are advertised.

Setup
Have students work in groups of four (preferably of mixed language ability), using the chart in Exercise 1 to record answers. Circulate among the groups, assisting with spelling and guiding discussion of questions in Exercise 2.

Expansion/Homework

Assign the discussion questions in Exercise 2 for writing. Ask the students to describe an advertisement that they often see or hear. Ask them to explain whether or not this advertisement makes them want to buy the product.

✪✪✪C PREPARING TO READ

BACKGROUND
Suggested Time: 10 minutes

Focus

To draw on students' background knowledge related to issues in global advertising that will be addressed in Reading One.

Setup

Have students (of different cultural backgrounds, if possible) work in small groups to decide if the statements are true or false. If they answer false, ask students to give reasons. Then ask them to edit the statements to make them true.

Expansion/Homework

Read all the statements together as a whole class, then assign individual statements to pairs of students and give them the responsibility of deciding if the statement is true or false. The pair must explain their decision to the class.

VOCABULARY FOR COMPREHENSION
Suggested Time: 20 minutes

Focus

To familiarize students with vocabulary that is commonly used to discuss the topic of advertising. These vocabulary items will appear in Reading One, so learning them will aid comprehension.

Setup

If possible, bring in a bottled water product and ask students to describe advertisements they have seen or heard for this type of product. Then pronounce each word and ask the students to repeat it. Discuss definitions, giving examples as needed. Point out that *market* is used as both a noun and a verb. Have the students complete the passage in pairs of different language ability, if possible. Go over the answers as a whole class.

Expansion/Homework

The exercise may be assigned as homework, as long as it is done before students begin Reading One.

2 Focus on Reading, PAGE 4

✪✪✪ A READING ONE: *Advertising All Over the World*

Suggested Time: 15 minutes 🕒

Focus
To help students anticipate the main ideas of the text by thinking about the problems faced by global advertisers.

Setup
Ask students to work with a partner to write down two or three possible problems that global advertisers might face, such as "language" or "misunderstanding." Ask the students to consider whether or not products that are successful in their home countries would be successful in other countries. Discuss the problems as a whole class. Then have students read the article.

Expansion/Homework
Ask students to consider the following question as well: *What might advertisers do to make their products marketable internationally?*

✪✪✪ READING FOR MAIN IDEAS
Suggested Time: 25 minutes 🕒

Focus
To give students an opportunity to demonstrate their understanding of the main ideas in the text.

Setup
Have the students confirm their answers in Section 1C (Preparing to Read, Background) and help them rewrite false statements to make them true. In writing short answers, have students practice the skill of incorporating the words and phrases of the questions into their answers.

Expansion/Homework
The exercises can be done as homework.

✪✪✪ READING FOR DETAILS
Suggested Time: 10 minutes 🕒

Focus
To confirm students' understanding of details and to reinforce important concepts such as marketing and communication.

Setup
Ask students to do the exercise in pairs, and then discuss their responses as a class. Encourage students to refer back to the text to confirm their answers. In question 5, explain to students that *custom* refers to a specific behavior, while *culture* is a broader concept that includes lifestyle, beliefs, and activities.

Expansion/Homework

This exercise can be done as a self-test. Have students complete the exercise individually and then go over the answers as a whole class.

✪✪ REACTING TO THE READING
Suggested Time: 25 minutes 🕐

Focus

To apply ideas from the text to a set of planned advertising campaigns; to support opinions using information from the text.

Setup

Read the campaign plans in items 1–3 as a whole class; make sure that students understand them. Have the students work in groups of three (of different language backgrounds, if possible) to decide whether or not each campaign will be successful. Make sure that the students support their opinions with information from the text. Encourage different opinions. Then have the students work in the same groups to answer items 4 and 5. Discuss the answers as a whole class.

Expansion/Homework

Assign the exercise as homework, and ask the students to answer items 1–3 by writing two or three sentences about each campaign.

Link to *NorthStar: Listening and Speaking*

Have students consider which of the planned ads would be most effective on the radio. Ask them how the radio ad might be changed in different world markets.

✪✪✪ B   READING TWO: *Changing World Markets*
Suggested Time: 15 minutes 🕐

Focus

To expand the topic of global advertising as students read a speech given by an advertising professional.

Setup

Read the introduction to the speech, and then discuss the introductory questions as a whole class. Be sensitive to political aspects of advertising in certain countries (for example, the use of posters and banners to display state slogans and images of leaders). It's best to read this article aloud or play the audio. While discussing it with the class, be sensitive to student food preferences, as the article raises the issue of food in different cultures. Have students identify the laws, customs, likes, and dislikes that advertisers must consider in Russia and China.

Expansion/Homework

Briefly explain each introductory question, and then ask students to choose one as a writing topic for homework.

✪✪✪ C   **LINKING READINGS ONE AND TWO**

Suggested Time: 20 minutes 🕐

Focus
To examine the changing markets in Russia and China and relate them to general problems of global advertising.

Setup
Assign the letter writing activity in Exercise 1 as individual homework. Then have the students work in pairs to complete the discussion questions in Exercise 2. Call on individual students to share their ideas with the whole class.

Expansion/Homework
(1) The questions in Exercise 2 can be assigned as writing topics, either before or after a general class discussion. (2) You can also ask students to exchange their letters and write a response from Ms. Ross.

3 Focus on Vocabulary, PAGE 12

✪ EXERCISE 1
Suggested Time: 10 minutes 🕐

Focus
To expand vocabulary studied in the unit by identifying appropriate synonyms.

Setup
Read the instructions and discuss the example. Have the students complete the exercise with a partner sitting nearby. Then go over the answers as a whole class. Be prepared to explain and give examples of each synonym as needed.

Expansion/Homework
This exercise can be assigned as homework and checked in class.

Link to *NorthStar: Listening and Speaking*
Play a vocabulary game. First, divide the class into two teams. Next, write vocabulary from Listening/Speaking Unit 1 on the board. Then award points for every synonym that students can think of. Allow students to question each other and disagree. At the end of the game, the team with the most points wins.

✪ EXERCISE 2
Suggested Time: 15 minutes 🕐

Focus
To examine the idioms used in Reading Two and to understand their meaning.

Setup
Read the definitions as a whole class, and provide explanations and examples as needed. Next, call on individual students to read items 1–8 aloud. Then have the

students work in pairs to match the definitions to the idioms. Go over the answers as a whole class.

Expansion/Homework

As a follow-up, personalize the activity by asking students to use the idioms to describe advertisements frequently seen in their local media community. (Example: I see advertisements for Pizza Hut *all over the place.*) First, do this orally, and then write their example sentences on the board. If possible, have students bring in advertisements to show to the class.

✪ EXERCISE 3
Suggested Time: 30 minutes

Focus

To give students an opportunity to create a commercial for TV or radio using a narrative or conversational format.

Setup

Go over the instructions with the class. Divide students into groups of three who work well together. Have them think first of a product and then of a format. Circulate among groups, offering help as needed. Check grammar before calling on each group to perform the commercial for the class.

Expansion/Homework

This activity could be videotaped and students could be encouraged to use props and realia.

For extra vocabulary practice, have students work on the self-grading vocabulary activities for the unit on the NorthStar Companion Website at **http://www.longman.com/northstar**.

4 Focus on Writing, PAGE 14

✪✪✪ A STYLE: Paragraph Development

Suggested Time: 25 minutes

Focus

This section lays the foundation for all paragraph writing that students will do in later units. It introduces the basic elements of a paragraph as well as indentation.

Setup

Have the students work in pairs to examine the paragraph in Exercise 1. Next, read the information about paragraph structure and present the examples. After this, identify the sentences in Exercise 2 as a whole class, and then have students work individually to combine the sentences into a paragraph that includes indentation. (If you prefer students to double-space their written work, now is the ideal time to teach this as well.)

Expansion/Homework

Provide additional practice by having students think of another product they use in daily life and generate a topic sentence, supporting details, and a concluding sentence. Do this as a whole class, and then have students combine the information into a doubled-spaced, indented paragraph.

✪✪B   GRAMMAR: Contrast—Simple Present and Present Progressive

Suggested Time: 20 minutes ⏱

Focus

To contrast the two present verb tenses in the context of fast-food advertising.

Setup

Have students read the sentences from Reading Two and compare the two verb tenses. Next, read the grammar explanations as a whole class, and answer any questions. Then have students test themselves by completing Exercise 2 individually. Go over the correct answers with the class, explaining problem items. Then have students complete Exercise 3 with a partner (of different language ability) before calling on individuals to share their ideas with the class.

Expansion/Homework

(1) Assign this section as homework. (2) For further practice, bring in pictures from magazine advertisements and have students work in pairs to describe them using both verb tenses. Ask, for example, *What is the person doing? How often do you think the person does this? What do you think the person believes about the product? Do you think this product is becoming more popular?* After students discuss the picture in pairs, have them write their sentences on the board for the whole class to review. (3) For further practice, offer exercises from *Focus on Grammar, Intermediate* and from *Fundamentals of English Grammar.* See the Grammar Book References on Student Book page 193 for specific units and chapters.

For extra practice in the writing process, have students go to the *NorthStar Writing Activity Book, Intermediate.*

✪✪✪C   WRITING TOPICS

Focus

To integrate the vocabulary, concepts, grammar (simple present/present progressive), and style focus (paragraph development) of the unit in a short writing assignment.

Setup

Discuss each question with the whole class, and use the board to keep track of student-generated ideas. Then assign the writing as homework, perhaps allowing several days. Remind students to use the vocabulary and style from this unit.

Expansion/Homework

Use samples of student writing to review grammar and/or vocabulary. Create an error correction exercise from sentences in which students misuse target verb tenses and/or words.

Link to *NorthStar: Listening and Speaking*

Encourage students to use vocabulary from Unit 1 in their writing.

✪D RESEARCH TOPIC

Focus

To take students into the real world of billboard advertising and to apply key concepts studied in the unit.

Setup

Assign each student the task of examining a billboard and completing the information in the worksheet. Then place students in small groups (preferably of mixed nationalities) and have them use the chart to record the ad's message, market, and potential for success. Encourage student discussion. Students may have insights to offer about each other's ads. Emphasize discussion Step 3 by having each group think of a different cultural context and determine how each ad would have to be changed to fit this market.

Expansion/Homework

Reinforce paragraph development by having each student choose one advertisement and write a paragraph describing its message, market, and potential for success. Provide a model for students to follow. Use student models to review paragraph development with the class.

Link to *NorthStar: Listening and Speaking*

This is an opportunity to ask students to apply the information about specific markets (gender, age, income) they worked with in Section 2A.

Going to Extremes: Sports and Obsession

OVERVIEW	
Theme:	Extreme sports

Readings:	*Interview with Tony Hawk*
	    An interview with a professional skateboarder
	High School Star Hospitalized for Eating Disorder
	    A newspaper report

Critical Thinking Skills:	Identify personal habits and attitudes Compare and contrast information gathered in a survey Infer meaning not explicit in text Analyze advantages and disadvantages of athletic obsession at an early age Compare and contrast two figures from two texts Interpret character motivation Draw conclusions based on information in the text
Reading Tasks:	Make predictions Read for main ideas Scan for details Underline important information in the text Relate text to personal experiences
Writing Tasks:	Write a factual report Write a personal reflection using new vocabulary Write an opinion response Compose interview questions Summarize interview in a factual report
Vocabulary:	Context clues Word forms Synonyms Vocabulary categorization
Grammar:	Modals of ability

UNIT SUMMARY

This unit deals with the psychological aspects of being obsessed with sports. Reading One is an interview with skateboarding star Tony Hawk. Reading Two is a newspaper article about a high school gymnast who is hospitalized with an eating disorder.

The companion unit in *NorthStar: Listening and Speaking* deals with pushing the limit in mountain climbing and other extreme sports.

1 Focus on the Topic, PAGE 19

✪✪✪ A PREDICTING

Suggested Time: 10 minutes

Focus
To get students thinking about dangerous sports by asking them to react to a photograph of a skier performing an aerial trick.

Setup
Have students read the title, look at the photo, and discuss the questions. Encourage all interpretations of the title.

Expansion/Homework
You may want to put the photograph (without the title or questions) on an overhead projector, if available. With books closed, have students study the photograph and write a paragraph describing it. Students can then write a title for the chapter based on the photograph and compare their ideas as a whole class. If you don't have access to an overhead projector, have students cover the title and questions and look at the photograph alone.

✪✪ B SHARING INFORMATION

Suggested Time: 20 minutes

Focus
To get students to pool information, experience, and vocabulary related to improving one's ability in sports.

Setup
After reading the introduction, divide the students into groups of four (of mixed fluency). Next, ask students to answer the questions and fill in the chart for themselves first before getting information from three other classmates. In the case that a student doesn't play a sport, ask him or her to talk about a hobby or interest instead. Then call on a spokesperson for each group to answer the items in Exercise 2. Compare the answers of each group to determine which classmate spends the most time practicing a sport and which one plays the most dangerous sport.

Expansion/Homework
For writing practice, you can have students summarize their completed charts in a paragraph.

✪✪✪ C PREPARING TO READ

BACKGROUND
Suggested Time: 10 minutes 🕐

Focus
To familiarize students with the concept of obsession by giving them a chance to learn more about the obsessions of great sports stars.

Setup
Read the introduction and then have the students work in pairs to do the matching exercise. Then have students compare their answers as a whole class.

Expansion/Homework
Encourage students to learn more about one of the stars by using the library and/or Internet to find photographs and biographical information. Students can then write a brief report on the star and share it with their classmates.

VOCABULARY FOR COMPREHENSION
Suggested Time: 15 minutes 🕐

Focus
To acquaint students with vocabulary that might typically be used in a discussion of extreme sports; to aid comprehension of Reading One.

Setup
Have students work individually to choose the word that best matches the meaning of the underlined word in each sentence. Then have them work with a classmate sitting nearby to compare answers. Go over the answers as a whole class.

Expansion/Homework
This exercise can be assigned as homework.

2 Focus on Reading, PAGE 22

✪✪✪ A READING ONE: *An Interview with Tony Hawk*
Suggested Time: 10 minutes 🕐

Focus
To spark students' curiosity about the reading and get them to anticipate ideas that will be presented in the text.

Setup

Ask students to write their questions individually. Then elicit questions from several students and write them on the board or on a transparency. Then have students read the interview, or play the tape as they read and listen.

Expansion/Homework

Have students work in pairs (of mixed fluency levels) to brainstorm questions.

✪✪✪ READING FOR MAIN IDEAS
Suggested Time: 10 minutes ⏲

Focus

To help students comprehend and identify main ideas in the text.

Setup

Have the students answer the questions individually and then check them with a partner sitting nearby.

Expansion/Homework

Have the students find the sentence or sentences in the reading that support each true and false answer. This can be done as homework. Then ask students to compare and discuss their answers in the next class.

✪✪✪ READING FOR DETAILS
Suggested Time: 20 minutes ⏲

Focus

To help students focus on relevant details in the text by answering a series of *wh-* questions.

Setup

Have students read the questions and write one-sentence answers. Then have students compare answers in pairs (of different fluency levels, if possible), referring back to the text when they disagree. Have volunteer students write their answers on the board.

Expansion/Homework

This exercise can be done as homework. Then ask students to compare and discuss their answers in the next class.

✪✪ REACTING TO THE READING
Suggested Time: 20 minutes ⏲

Focus

To practice inference skills by having students select information from the text to complete a dialogue; to give students a chance to consider the pros and cons of being a young athlete.

Setup

Read the instructions and dialogue in Exercise 1. Then have students work in pairs (of mixed fluency levels) to complete the dialogue with information from the text. Based on their understanding of the text, encourage them to guess what Tony Hawk's parents would probably say. For Exercise 2, divide the students into small groups (of mixed fluency levels) to discuss and list the good and bad points of being a young athlete. Circulate among groups to offer help as needed and then call on each group to share its ideas with the class.

Expansion/Homework

Exercises 1 and 2 can both be done as homework, with class time used for students to discuss their answers in small groups (of varying fluency levels).

Link to *NorthStar: Listening and Speaking*

Add the following questions to students' discussion in Exercise 2: *Do you think minors (under age 18) should be allowed to do dangerous sports? What kind of age limit do you think is fair for sports such as mountain climbing, bungee jumping, and skydiving? What are the good and bad points of having an age limit?*

✪✪✪ B   READING TWO: *High School Star Hospitalized for Eating Disorder*

Suggested Time: 30 minutes

Focus

To contrast the success that Tony Hawk found through his skateboarding obsession with the tragic illness faced by an athlete as a result of her gymnastics obsession.

Setup

If possible, bring in pictures of gymnasts and discuss the requirements of the sport (agility, balance, strength, dedication). Next, with books closed, write the title of the unit on the board and ask the students to consider how a gymnastics star might develop an eating disorder. Make sure that they understand the concept of "anorexia" before they read. Then have them work in pairs (of mixed fluency levels) to answer the questions. Go over the answers as a whole class. Then have students read the article.

Expansion/Homework

(1) Exercises 1 and 2 can be done as homework, with class time used to review answers and discuss the text. (2) For more writing practice, you can have the students write a letter of encouragement to Ashley Lindermann focusing on her potential for success.

Link to *NorthStar: Listening and Speaking*

Review the concept of "sensation seeker" and ask them to describe the sensations that people such as Tony Hawk and Ashley Lindermann are seeking.

✪✪✪ C **LINKING READINGS ONE AND TWO**

Suggested Time: 25 minutes

Focus
To have students use information from both readings to compare the obsessions of two athletes; to consider various factors that result in an obsession with sports.

Setup
For Exercise 1, ask students to work in small groups (of mixed fluency levels) to answer the questions. Make sure they support their answers with information from the texts. Encourage a wide variety of answers as long as students' reasoning is sound. For Exercise 2, read the introduction and do the first item together as an example. Have students complete the exercise individually before comparing answers in pairs (of mixed fluency levels.) Then go over each item on the list and call on various pairs to comment. Elicit as many other reasons for obsession as possible and encourage students to share real-life examples of people developing obsessions for those reasons.

Expansion/Homework
(1) For more writing practice, assign item A in Exercise 1 as a writing assignment for homework. Have the students write one or two paragraphs comparing the two athletes and commenting on the role that obsession has played in their lives. Use class time for having students read their paragraphs in pairs. Then collect them to assess the depth of students' comprehension and analysis of the readings.
(2) Exercise 2 can be done as homework, with class time used for class discussion.

❸ Focus on Vocabulary, PAGE 28

✪ EXERCISE 1
Suggested Time: 15 minutes

Focus
To review vocabulary from the unit by working with various word forms.

Setup
Ask students to complete the exercise and then compare answers with a classmate sitting nearby, discussing any answers that are different. Encourage them to use dictionaries as needed.

Expansion/Homework
This exercise can be done as homework, with class time used to check answers.

Link to *NorthStar: Listening and Speaking*
Encourage students to think of related word forms for the Unit 2 vocabulary items.

✪ EXERCISE 2
Suggested Time: 15 minutes

Focus

To give students a chance to use vocabulary from the unit in a new context.

Setup

Have students look at the photo of Gelsey Kirkland and discuss the skills and attributes required to be a dancer. Then read the cloze passage aloud before having students fill in the blanks. Remind them that they may need to change the forms of words. Then go over the answers as a whole class.

Expansion/Homework

(1) This exercise can be assigned as homework. (2) Students can complete this assignment in pairs (of mixed fluency levels.)

✪ EXERCISE 3
Suggested Time: 25 minutes

Focus

To give students a chance to use the new vocabulary by writing about their own accomplishments in sports or other areas.

Setup

Read the instructions and brainstorm examples of each type of accomplishment. Then give students time to write in class. Circulate among students and offer help with word usage. Collect the paragraphs and use them to assess student ability to use the new words correctly.

Expansion/Homework

(1) This assignment can be done as homework, with class time used to share paragraphs in small groups. (2) Collect the paragraphs and use them to create an error correction worksheet focusing on word usage errors.

 For extra vocabulary practice, have students work on the self-grading vocabulary activities for the unit on the NorthStar Companion Website at **http://www.longman.com/northstar**.

4 Focus on Writing, PAGE 30

✪✪✪ A   STYLE: Writing a Factual Report
Suggested Time: 30 minutes

Focus

To build skill in writing factual reports based on the 5 Ws: who, what, when, where, why or how.

Setup

Read the introduction and have students review the newspaper article in Reading Two. Then read the explanation of the 5 Ws and offer clarification as needed. Have students complete Exercises 2 and 3 individually before sharing their paragraphs with a partner sitting nearby. Call on a few students to share their paragraphs with the whole class and make sure that students understand the important facts. Then do Exercise 4 as a whole class before having students work individually to write a factual report.

Expansion/Homework

(1) This section can be assigned as homework. (2) For more practice, you can have students bring in sports articles from their local newspaper. Then have them work in small groups to use the 5 Ws to write factual reports based on the articles.

Link to *NorthStar: Listening and Speaking*

Have students use the 5 Ws to identify the main facts from Listening One and then use these facts to write a factual report.

✪✪B   GRAMMAR: Modals of Ability

Suggested Time: 25 minutes

Focus

To learn about modals of ability and to use them in the context of a personal letter.

Setup

Have students look at the examples from Reading One and explain the meaning of the underlined words. Next, read the information in the chart before having students complete Exercise 2 individually. Then have students check their answers with a partner sitting nearby. Go over the answers as a whole class.

Expansion/Homework

(1) This section can be assigned as homework. (2) If you have an overhead projector, place the exercise on a transparency for easier correction and review. (3) For further practice, offer exercises from *Focus on Grammar Intermediate* and from *Fundamentals of English Grammar*. See the Grammar Book References on Student Book page 193 for specific units and chapters.

 For extra practice in the writing process, have students go to the *NorthStar Writing Activity Book, Intermediate*.

✪✪✪C   WRITING TOPICS

Focus

To integrate the vocabulary, concepts, grammar (modals of ability), and style focus (writing a factual report) of the unit in a short writing assignment.

Setup
Discuss the topics in class and assign the writing as homework, perhaps allowing several days.

Expansion/Homework
(1) You might have students pair up and read each other's papers, discussing what they liked about their partner's paper and what was confusing or difficult to understand. (2) If students have access to PowerPoint technology, they can use it to give presentations on Topic 1.

✪D RESEARCH TOPIC

Focus
To take the students into the real world of sports by having them write a factual report on the accomplishments of an individual or team.

Setup
Read the instructions and make sure students understand the 5 Ws that they must include in their report. Help them think of individuals or teams in their community that they can interview. Direct them to newspapers and websites they can use for more research. After the students have prepared their reports, have them work in small groups (of mixed fluency levels) to read their reports to each other and choose the most interesting report to share with the class.

Expansion/Homework
Students can use the 5 Ws to write interview questions for a guest speaker (a local sports or dance figure). Then they can use the interview findings to write a factual report on the speaker.

Link to *NorthStar: Listening and Speaking*
Encourage students to find someone who has "pushed the limit" by participating in a high-risk sports activity. Students can use the 5 Ws to report on this person. Also, encourage them to use vocabulary from Unit 2.

Miracle Cure?

OVERVIEW	
Theme:	Fraud

Readings:	*A Miracle Cure?*
	    A magazine article
	The Organic Health Center
	    An advertisement

Critical Thinking Skills:	Analyze an advertisement Make judgments Evaluate information according to criteria set forth in a text Correlate information from two texts Compare and contrast medical treatments Critique advertisements
Reading Tasks:	Make predictions Read for main ideas Locate information in a text Support answers with evidence from the text Read for details Relate supporting details to main ideas Summarize the readings
Writing Tasks:	Compose a summary paragraph Organize information within a paragraph Write topic sentences Identify and use transitions in a paragraph Report information gathered in an interview Write an advertisement Summarize research findings
Vocabulary:	Word definitions Context clues Prefixes and suffixes
Grammar:	Superlative adjectives

UNIT SUMMARY

This unit focuses on how quacks work, why people trust quacks, and how to recognize a quack. Reading One is an article from a popular magazine warning people about quacks. Reading Two is an advertisement for a quack who specializes in "curing" cancer.

The companion unit in *NorthStar: Listening and Speaking* deals with telemarketing fraud and how con artists manipulate their victims

1 Focus on the Topic, PAGE 35

✪✪✪A PREDICTING

Suggested Time: 10 minutes 🕐

Focus
To get students thinking about false and fraudulent advertising by asking them to react to a typical ad that promotes a miracle cure product.

Setup
Ask students to read the title and the advertisement. Explain any vocabulary in the ad that they don't understand. Give students a minute or two to think about their answers to the predicting questions. Elicit responses, and write them on the board. Ask if other students agree or disagree.

Expansion/Homework
Students could prepare their answers in small groups (of different cultural backgrounds, if possible) and then report back to the class.

✪✪B SHARING INFORMATION

Suggested Time: 25 minutes 🕐

Focus
To discover the real experience students have had with quackery; to raise students' consciousness of how common these treatments are and how we can all be victims of false advertising.

Setup
Ask students to read the items in the chart. Have pairs (of different language backgrounds, if possible) interview each other about their own experience or that of someone they know. Elicit questions to ask in the interview and write them on the board (for example, *What about an herb tea to cure colds? Have you ever seen an ad for it? Have you used it? Do you know someone who has? Did it work?*). Then have students share examples of the most interesting stories with the class. Ask for the class's reactions.

Expansion/Homework

Use the chart to conduct a class survey. Have students mingle in the classroom, trying to find someone who has had an experience with a particular product. Discuss the most unusual situation found in this survey.

Link to *NorthStar: Listening and Speaking*

Have students discuss whether they have had any experience with telemarkers selling health or weight-loss products.

✪✪✪ C   PREPARING TO READ

BACKGROUND
Suggested Time: 15 minutes

Focus

To introduce students to the alarming facts about quackery in the United States. The questions that follow the fact list are meant to stimulate students' thinking about why the facts are true. Students can draw on their background knowledge to answer these questions.

Setup

Read the facts aloud to the class. Next, have students work in pairs (of different cultural backgrounds, if possible) to discuss their answers to the questions in Exercises 1 and 2. Then have students discuss their opinions as a whole class.

Expansion/Homework

Discuss the questions in Exercise 2 as a class. Elicit opinions from the students and write their ideas on the board. Then ask volunteers to agree or disagree with the responses.

Link to *NorthStar: Listening and Speaking*

Ask students to consider why elderly people are victims of not only telemarketing but also health fraud. Have them write their answers in class or as homework.

VOCABULARY FOR COMPREHENSION
Suggested Time: 20 minutes

Focus

To acquaint students with vocabulary that is typically used in discussions of quackery; to aid comprehension of Reading One.

Setup

Students should work individually to answer the multiple-choice questions. Encourage them to determine meaning through context clues. As they finish, they can compare their answers with another student sitting nearby. Then they can discuss the answers with the whole class.

Expansion/Homework

(1) Assign the exercise as homework and use class time to review the answers. In class, have students compare their answers with those of a partner and then check the answers with you. (2) To encourage more discussion of vocabulary, have the students complete this exercise in pairs (of mixed language ability).

✷✷✷ 2 Focus on Reading, PAGE 39

✸✸✸ A   READING ONE: *A Miracle Cure?*
Suggested Time: 5 minutes ⏱

Focus
To help students predict the content of the magazine article.

Setup
Conduct a class discussion of the title and questions. You may want to write students' ideas on the board. The use of a question in the title is meant to imply that there is no such thing as a miracle cure. Encourage students to share examples of "miracle cures" from their own cultures.

Expansion/Homework
(1) Have students work in small groups (of varying fluency levels) to answer the questions. Then call on each group to share ideas with the class. (2) The pre-reading questions can be used as a brief in-class writing assignment. (3) The reading can be assigned as homework.

✪✪✪ READING FOR MAIN IDEAS
Suggested Time: 20 minutes ⏱

Focus
To identify the main ideas in the text; to identify specific parts of the text where main ideas are explicit.

Setup
Have students read the questions and possible answers first. Ask if there is anything they don't understand. Clarify unknown vocabulary in the six questions and answers. Have students answer the questions as they read.

Expansion/Homework
This section could be assigned as homework.

✪✪✪ READING FOR DETAILS
Suggested Time: 15 minutes ⏱

Focus
To help students complete sentences using detailed information from the text; to relate details to the main ideas.

Setup

Have students complete the matching. Then have students compare their answers in pairs (of different fluency levels, if possible), referring back to the text when there is disagreement.

Expansion/Homework

You may want to have the students complete this exercise at home. Then ask students to compare and discuss their answers in class.

✪✪ REACTING TO THE READING
Suggested Time: 25 minutes 🕐

Focus

To give students a chance to think critically about information they learned from Reading One; to consider what they would do if they were victims of health fraud.

Setup

Read the instructions and have students complete Exercise 1 in pairs before forming groups (of mixed language levels) to discuss their answers. Check with each group to see if there are any points of disagreement. Encourage disagreement as long as students' reasoning is sound. Next, have each group divide into pairs to discuss the questions in Exercise 2. Then call on individual students to share their ideas with the class.

Expansion/Homework

(1) Question 1 in Exercise 2 can be given as a writing assignment. (2) In response to question 2 in Exercise 2, students can work in small groups to think of an example of health fraud. Then they can write a letter to a government agency in the role of a health fraud victim. In their letters, they should describe what happened and ask the agency to take action.

✪✪✪ B   READING TWO: *The Organic Health Center*
Suggested Time: 10–15 minutes 🕐

Focus

To extend the topic of quackery as students read an advertisement written by a quack.

Setup

Ask students to read the text individually in class. As they finish reading, have them work in pairs (of mixed language ability) to answer the questions that follow the text. Go over the answers with the whole class.

Expansion/Homework

(1) To encourage use of the unit vocabulary, list useful words on the board and have students use them in their discussion. (2) You may want to assign the reading and Exercise 2 as homework. Then have students compare their answers with a partner sitting nearby. Finally, go over the answers as a whole class.

Link to *NorthStar: Listening and Speaking*
Have students write a paragraph listing three reasons why Benjamin Harrison is a con artist.

✪✪✪ C   LINKING READINGS ONE AND TWO

Suggested Time: 25 minutes 🕐

Focus

To have students analyze a real example of a quack selling his product and relate it to the general discussion of quackery and how to identify it.

Setup

Ask students to work in small groups (of varying fluency levels) to fill in the chart in Exercise 1 with information from both readings. Appoint a "secretary" to write down the examples group members find. Then go over the answers together. Next, have students work in pairs (of different cultural backgrounds, if possible) to answer Exercise 2. Encourage students to answer these questions based on their own cultural values about medicine. Reviewing this exercise as a whole class should lead to a lively class discussion.

Expansion/Homework

You may want to ask students to fill in the chart individually before they discuss it with classmates. This could be done as homework.

Link to *NorthStar: Listening and Speaking*
Add this question: *How are quacks similar to fraudulent telemarketers?*

❸ Focus on Vocabulary, PAGE 44

✪ EXERCISE 1

Suggested Time: 15 minutes 🕐

Focus

To make students aware of how prefixes and suffixes are used to derive new word meanings.

Setup

Have students read the sentences from Reading One and discuss the questions. Next, read the explanation before having students look at the list and circle words that have a negative meaning. Then ask students to think of words from this unit that can be changed into new words by using prefixes and/or suffixes. Write the words on the board for students to copy in their books.

Link to *NorthStar: Listening and Speaking*
Have students think of words from Unit 3 that can be changed into new words by using prefixes and/or suffixes.

✪ EXERCISE 2
Suggested Time: 15 minutes

Focus
To reinforce vocabulary studied in the unit in new contexts.

Setup
Read the instructions and ask students to write the sentences individually. As they finish writing their sentences, invite them to compare their answers with a classmate (sitting nearby) before going over the answers as a whole class.

Expansion/Homework
You could assign this exercise as homework.

✪ EXERCISE 3
Suggested Time: 25 minutes

Focus
To move beyond a passive knowledge of the vocabulary studied in the unit to an active knowledge as students use the words in original expression.

Setup
Read the instructions and go over the example. Next, have students work in pairs (of different fluency levels, if possible). Student A will choose four words from the first column and use them to write four questions. Student B will choose four words from the second column and use them to write four questions. You might want to wander around the room, offering comments and suggestions when students' questions aren't clear. Then have the partners exchange papers and write answers to each other's questions. Ask students to try to use a word from either column in each of their answers. As they finish writing their answers, invite them to discuss their questions and answers with their partners.

Expansion/Homework
Keep the written dialogue going. Ask students to continue writing questions and answers to each other as a conversation.

Link to *NorthStar: Listening and Speaking*
List the vocabulary from Unit 3 and have students choose from those words as well.

 For extra vocabulary practice, have students work on the self-grading vocabulary activities for the unit on the NorthStar Companion Website at **http://www.longman.com/northstar**.

4 Focus on Writing, PAGE 47

✪✪✪ A STYLE: Summary Writing

Suggested Time: 40 minutes ⏱

Focus

To guide students as they write a summary of a familiar text, using a topic sentence and transitions.

Setup

For Exercise 1, it would be helpful to use an overhead transparency to allow students to view Reading Two while they look at the summary in their books. Read the summary to the class and ask students to explain how it is different from the original text. Next, read the explanatory information in the shaded box. Then have the students work individually to complete Exercise 2 before reviewing it as a whole class. Once the correct order has been established, ask students to write the summary on a separate sheet of paper. Then read the instructions for Exercise 3 and have students write summaries individually. Circulate among students and offer help as needed.

Expansion/Homework

(1) Exercise 3 can be done as homework. When students return to class, have them exchange summaries with a partner and check each other's work for the use of transition words. Then collect the summaries and use the best ones as examples for the class. (2) For additional practice, have students find articles about health and/or fraud. Next, have them write summaries of these articles using the guidelines provided in this unit. Be sure to have them submit the original text with their summaries for your comments and review. (Another option is for you to provide one article for all students to summarize.)

✪✪ B GRAMMAR: Adjectives—Superlatives

Suggested Time: 30 minutes ⏱

Focus

To use superlative adjectives to compare fraudulent products in advertisements.

Setup

Have students compare the pairs of sentences and discuss the differences. Next, read the explanatory information and the chart. Encourage students to share what they already know about this form. Then have students complete Exercise 2 individually before going over the answers with the class.

Expansion/Homework

(1) This whole section works well as homework. Use class time to check answers and provide clarification as needed. (2) For further practice, offer exercises from *Focus on Grammar, Intermediate* and from *Fundamentals of English Grammar*.

See the Grammar Book References on Student Book page 193 for specific units and chapters.

 For extra practice in the writing process, have students go to the *NorthStar Writing Activity Book, Intermediate.*

WRITING TOPICS

Focus
To integrate the vocabulary, concepts, grammar (superlative adjectives), and style focus (summary writing) of the unit in a short writing assignment.

Setup
Assign this exercise for homework, perhaps allowing several days. Encourage the students to use the vocabulary, grammar, and style from this unit in their writing.

Expansion/Homework
Use samples of student writing to review grammar before they begin this assignment. If possible, create an error correction exercise from sentences in which students misuse the superlative.

Link to *NorthStar: Listening and Speaking*
Ask students to use vocabulary and grammar from Unit 3 in their writing.

RESEARCH TOPIC

Focus
To take the students into the real world of fraudulent advertising; to reinforce the skill of summary writing.

Setup
Bring in many examples of magazines (particularly fashion and health magazines). You can also ask students to bring in magazines to share. Next, have students work in small groups (of different cultural backgrounds, if possible) to find advertisements that might be fraudulent. Appoint one student to write down information about the advertisement and to record student ideas about what kind of person might buy the product. Next, have a spokesperson from each group visit another group and present a report on the selected product. Then ask students to summarize their group's report individually.

Expansion/Homework
Students can also be assigned to find fraudulent health claims on the Internet. These articles or advertisements can be brought in for small-group use.

Link to *Northstar: Listening and Speaking*
Encourage students to use the grammar and vocabulary from Unit 3 in their discussion and writing. You can also add the following questions to the small-group discussion: *Do you think this product could be sold by a telemarketer? Do you think this product is an example of something that might be sold by a con artist to elderly people?*

The Metamorphosis

OVERVIEW	
Theme:	Storytelling

Readings:	*The Metamorphosis*
	    An abridged story
	Ungeziefer
	    A critique of the story

Critical Thinking Skills:	Recognize personal assumptions Infer word meaning from context Examine symbol and imagery in a text Contrast different points of view in a text Interpret characters' emotions
Reading Tasks:	Make predictions Paraphrase main ideas Support answers with information from the text Connect generalizations to specific passages Locate information in the text Compare personal reactions to a critique Retell a short story with an illustration Research the metamorphosis process
Writing Tasks:	Paraphrase sentences Write statements of purpose Compose a short story Write an opinion paragraph Paraphrase research in a report and use a diagram to relate facts
Vocabulary:	Word definitions Synonyms Context clues Comparison and contrast of word meaning and usage
Grammar:	Infinitives of purpose Relative pronouns

UNIT SUMMARY

This unit examines our attitudes toward insects through an abridged version of Kafka's "The Metamorphosis," a story in which a man wakes up to discover he has become a cockroach. Reading One is the abridged story. Reading Two is what critics have said about the story.

The companion unit in *NorthStar: Listening and Speaking* explores the art of storytelling; it includes an interview with a master storyteller and a presentation of one of her stories.

1 Focus on the Topic, PAGE 53

✪✪✪ A PREDICTING

Suggested Time: 10 minutes

Focus
To get students to express their thoughts and feelings about insects by asking them to react to a picture of a cockroach and brainstorm descriptive vocabulary.

Setup
Using the illustration in the book, have students brainstorm two lists: adjectives that describe the cockroach and adjectives that describe their feelings about cockroaches. Ask students to share their lists as you write them on the board or on a transparency for an overhead projector.

Expansion/Homework
(1) You can put the illustration on an overhead projector, if available. (2) You could help students with vocabulary by listing some words on the board, for example, *yucky, gross, icky, weird, goosebumps*, and so on. (3) This activity could be done as a homework assignment. In class, the students could share their lists in groups, and you could write them on the board. You could then have students identify the words that have positive and negative connotations to get them to focus on people's varying attitudes about insects.

✪✪ B SHARING INFORMATION

Suggested Time: 20 minutes

Focus
To give students a chance to share their experiences with insects; to increase their awareness of insects as a source of both disgust and fascination.

Setup
Have the students get into groups (of different cultural backgrounds, if possible) and discuss the questions. Circulate among groups and offer help with

vocabulary as needed. Also, listen for interesting anecdotes, information, or vocabulary that can be shared with the whole class.

Expansion/Homework

You might have the students pick one or two of the questions to write about as homework. In class, students can exchange papers with a classmate and read each other's responses.

✪✪✪ C PREPARING TO READ

BACKGROUND
Suggested Time: 15 minutes

Focus

To make students aware of the personality and background of the author so that, later, they will be more able to make connections between the author and Gregor, the main character in the story.

Setup

Have students look at the picture of Franz Kafka. Then read the paragraph to the class before having students work in pairs (of different fluency levels) to discuss the questions. Then call on individual students to share their ideas with the class. Allow disagreement as long as students' reasoning is sound.

Expansion/Homework

(1) This exercise could be assigned as homework, with class time used for discussion. (2) You might bring in a large map and have the students locate Prague, Kafka's home city. (3) After students have discussed the questions, you can have them create a role play. Divide the class into groups of three (of varying fluency levels) and have members of the group take on the roles of Kafka and his parents. Give them the following situation: *The family is having dinner together and Kafka tells his parents that he has changed his mind about getting married. His parents are disappointed, and they start to argue with their son.* (4) After students have discussed the questions, have them follow up by researching the life of Franz Kafka in more detail. Have them write a brief summary of their research and share it with the class.

VOCABULARY FOR COMPREHENSION
Suggested Time: 25 minutes

Focus

To introduce the vocabulary that students will encounter in Reading One to aid comprehension of the text.

Setup

For Exercise 1, students should work individually and without their dictionaries to guess the meanings of the words from context. You may want to do the first item together as an example. Next, have students compare their answers as a whole class. Then have students do Exercise 2 individually before comparing answers with a partner sitting nearby. Then go over the answers as a whole class.

Expansion/Homework
(1) This section could be assigned as homework, with class time used to check answers. (2) After students complete this section, you can play a game. First, have students close their books and write as many of the words as they can in two minutes. Then have one student write his or her words on the board. Other students can offer correction as needed.

2 Focus on Reading, PAGE 57

✪✪✪ A   READING ONE: *The Metamorphosis*
Suggested Time: 15 minutes ⏲

Focus
To get students motivated to read by asking them to predict the content of the story.

Setup
Have students look at the picture of the cockroach on page 53 and then read the paragraph. Then have students read and discuss the questions in pairs (of varying fluency levels). Next, call on pairs to share their ideas with the class. Encourage a variety of answers.

Expansion/Homework
For more writing practice, you can have students write a paragraph in which they answer questions 1 and 2. Note that question 1 requires the use of the past tense and question 2 requires the use of *would* as the past of *will*, so you may need to give a brief explanation. This could be done as homework. In the next class, have students exchange papers, read them, and discuss any differences. Then have students read the story.

Link to *NorthStar: Listening and Speaking*
Ask students to volunteer to tell other stories or fables that involve sleeping and/or dreaming.

✪✪✪ READING FOR MAIN IDEAS
Suggested Time: 20 minutes ⏲

Focus
To help students comprehend the global meaning of the text.

Setup
Have students scan the questions for any vocabulary they don't understand. Then have the students work individually or with a partner to correct the main ideas. They can write their answers on the board. Ask the class to read the answers, looking for any that are different from their own and discussing any

differences. Refer to sections in the text where information can be found to correct the statements.

Expansion/Homework

(1) After finishing the activity, you might want to ask the students if the main ideas are in order or not. (They are.) (2) Students could also write the answers as homework and review the answers in class. (3) For more writing practice, you could have the students write the corrected main ideas in a paragraph as a summary. Review the point that a summary is a shorter version of a story because it contains only main ideas.

✪✪✪ READING FOR DETAILS
Suggested Time: 20 minutes ⏱

Focus

To get students to examine the text more thoroughly by looking for details that have been paraphrased.

Setup

Have students read the instructions and do the exercise individually. As students finish writing, have them work with a partner sitting nearby to compare answers. Elicit answers, discussing any that are incorrect or confusing to students.

Expansion/Homework

(1) This exercise could be done as homework. (2) You might want to extend this exercise by asking students to identify the words in the paraphrased sentence that differ from the original. Point out that knowing a lot of synonyms is a helpful skill in paraphrasing; you might want to mention how paraphrasing can be used to avoid plagiarism.

✪✪ REACTING TO THE READING
Suggested Time: 30–40 minutes ⏱

Focus

To get students to move beyond the literal meaning of the story to interpret and infer.

Setup

Read the instructions for Exercise 1 and have students complete it individually. Next, have students compare their answers with a partner sitting nearby. Discuss any differences as a whole class. For Exercise 2, read the questions and have students respond individually on a separate sheet of paper. Be sure to have them review their predictions in Section 2A and compare them to the story. Call on individual students to share their ideas with the class.

Expansion/Homework

(1) This exercise could be assigned as homework. (2) For more writing practice, have partners read each other's answers and check for specific errors. For example, you could review the rules for two or three conjunctions, such as *and,*

but, and *so,* and then have the students check their partners' answers for this type of error. Then do a final check to be sure corrections are done properly.

Link to *NorthStar: Listening and Speaking*
Ask students to tell stories involving insects, transformation, and/or the breakdown of family ties.

✪✪✪ B   READING TWO: *Ungeziefer*

Suggested Time: 20 minutes ⏲

Focus
To stimulate critical thinking as students read critics' opinions of Kafka and "The Metamorphosis."

Setup
If possible, bring in a book review section of a newspaper and discuss the role of literary critics. Then read the introduction and explain the title "Ungeziefer" **/un gɛ 'tsi fær/** before having students read the text on their own. Next, read the questions in Exercise 2 and have students write their answers individually. Then discuss the answers as a whole class.

Expansion/Homework
You might want to have students collaborate on Exercise 2 in pairs of different fluency levels.

✪✪✪ C   LINKING READINGS ONE AND TWO

Suggested Time: 25 minutes ⏲

Focus
To get students to arrive at a deeper understanding of the topic and exercise critical thinking skills by distinguishing different points of view: their viewpoints, their classmates' viewpoints, and the critics' viewpoints.

Setup
Read the instructions, and then have students take the paper with the answers they wrote in Exercise 2 of Reacting to the Reading and lay it next to the page with answers they wrote about the critics in the previous section. This will allow them to compare their ideas about the story with those of the critics. Next, students can compare their answers with those of their classmates in small groups (of different cultural backgrounds, if possible). Then ask students to work as a whole class to discuss whether students or critics were more critical of Gregor and his story.

Expansion/Homework
You could have the students write a paragraph comparing their responses to those of the critics. Next, students could share their writing in small groups (of different cultural backgrounds, if possible) and discuss their differing opinions.

3 Focus on Vocabulary, PAGE 64

✪ EXERCISES 1 AND 2
Suggested Time: 15 minutes ⏱

Focus
To give students a chance to explore variations in meaning created by synonyms.

Setup
Have students look at the pairs of sentences in item 1. Read the explanation of synonyms and elicit more examples. Next, read the instructions to Exercise 2 and do the first item together as an example before having students complete the exercise individually. Then call on individual students to share their answers. When there is variation in meaning, offer explanation as needed.

Expansion/Homework
This section can be done as homework and reviewed in class.

Link to *NorthStar: Listening and Speaking*
Select some vocabulary words from Unit 4 and have students find synonyms with more general or specific meanings.

✪ EXERCISE 3
Suggested Time: 15 minutes ⏱

Focus
To review vocabulary from the unit in the context of a crossword puzzle.

Setup
Make sure that students understand how to complete the puzzle. Then have them solve it individually or with a partner sitting nearby. If possible, use an overhead transparency to review the completed puzzle.

Expansion/Homework
(1) The puzzle can be done as homework and reviewed in class. (2) You can divide the class into two teams and award a small prize to the team that completes the puzzle first.

Link to *NorthStar: Listening and Speaking*
Divide the class into two or more teams. Have them choose vocabulary from Unit 4 and challenge each other by creating crossword puzzles for their classmates to solve.

✪ EXERCISE 4
Suggested Time: 25 minutes ⏱

Focus
To give the students a chance to use vocabulary from the unit in original written expression.

Setup

Read the questions and make sure students understand them. Then give the students time to write their answers individually. Circulate among students and make sure they are using the underlined words in their responses. When students are finished writing, have volunteers write their sentences on the board. Discuss each sentence and correct word usage as needed.

Expansion/Homework

This activity can be done as homework and submitted to you for evaluation. Use errors as a springboard for discussing correct word usage. You may wish to prepare an error correction worksheet for the class.

Link to *NorthStar: Listening and Speaking*

Have students write two questions of their own using the vocabulary from Unit 4. Then have partners exchange questions and write their answers in class or as homework.

 For extra vocabulary practice, have students work on the self-grading vocabulary activities for the unit on the NorthStar Companion Website at **http://www.longman.com/northstar**.

4 Focus on Writing, PAGE 68

✪✪✪ A   STYLE: Paraphrasing

Suggested Time: 25 minutes

Focus

To help students develop skills in paraphrasing as they paraphrase sentences from the story.

Setup

Begin by writing *I love my job* on the board. Ask students to express the same idea using different words. Next, read the explanation, and then have students complete Exercise 1 with a partner sitting nearby. You might want to help them see the value of paraphrasing by explaining its importance in writing summaries and reports. Next, have students do Exercise 2 individually. Circulate among students, offering encouragement and suggesting alternatives as needed. Then have several volunteers write their paraphrases on the board and offer comments and corrections.

Expansion/Homework

You might want to assign Exercise 2 for homework. In class, you could have several students write their paraphrases on the board. Then discuss what worked well, what didn't work well, and why.

Link to *NorthStar: Listening and Speaking*
The biography in Section 1C (Background) could be paraphrased by students in small groups, written on the board, and corrected.

✪✪B   GRAMMAR: Infinitives of Purpose

Suggested Time: 25 minutes

Focus
To use infinitives of purpose to explain why characters in "The Metamorphosis" behaved as they did.

Setup
Have students work in pairs to examine the example sentences in Exercise 1, underline the infinitive verbs, and discuss the questions these verbs answer. Encourage students to share what they know about this form. Then have them refer to the grammar explanations as they work independently to complete Exercise 2. Go over the answers as a whole class, and then have students complete Exercise 3 individually before comparing answers with a partner sitting nearby. Then have volunteers put their sentences on the board, and offer any necessary feedback or correction.

Expansion/Homework
(1) This section works well as homework. You could use class time for peer correction of student sentences written on the board. (2) For further practice, offer exercises from *Focus on Grammar, Intermediate* and from *Fundamentals of English Grammar*. See the Grammar Book References on Student Book page 193 for specific units and chapters.

Link to *NorthStar: Listening and Speaking*
Students can work in teams to write questions about the story "Lavender." Students on other teams can win points by answering the questions using infinitives of purpose.

 For extra practice in the writing process, have students go to the *NorthStar Writing Activity Book, Intermediate*.

✪✪✪C   WRITING TOPICS

Focus
To integrate the vocabulary, concepts, grammar (infinitives of purpose), and style focus (paraphrasing) of the unit in a short writing assignment.

Setup
Assign this exercise for homework, perhaps allowing several days.

Expansion/Homework

You could have the students share their writing in small groups. Facilitate peer feedback by directing students to comment on both content (what they enjoyed reading) and form (use of vocabulary and style). Also, encourage students to write one or two questions about the content. Make sure that students are able to read all their peer comments.

✪D RESEARCH TOPICS

Focus

To extend students' knowledge by giving them a chance to read another story or conduct research on metamorphosis.

Setup

For Topic 1, you can aid story selection by arranging for students to visit a library or bookstore. You can increase student interest by giving your own presentation, including an illustration. For Topic 2, direct students to encyclopedias, science books, or the Internet. Remind students of the importance of paraphrasing information in order to avoid plagiarism.

Expansion/Homework

(1) For Topic 1, you might want to encourage students to read fairy tales or children's books. These provide a rich variety of material related to animals, including insects. (2) If students have access to PowerPoint technology, they can use it to enhance their presentations.

Speaking of Gender

OVERVIEW	
Theme:	Language

Readings:	*Different Ways of Talking*
	    An article
	Speaking of Gender
	    An interview with a linguist

Critical Thinking Skills:	Assess gender-typing in own culture Identify personal assumptions about gender Infer information not explicit in the text Support a personal opinion with examples from the text Evaluate speech according to criteria set forth in a text Synthesize information from two readings Analyze gender influence in speech and behavior
Reading Tasks:	Make predictions Read for main ideas Locate details in the text Relate text to one's own observations
Writing Tasks:	Write sentences with transitions to compare and contrast Write requests in correspondence Compose paragraphs to compare and contrast gender roles and behavior Take observation notes of a TV program Write a paragraph summary of research findings
Vocabulary:	Synonyms Context clues Vocabulary classification
Grammar:	Using modals for requests

UNIT SUMMARY

This unit explores the way in which gender affects language. Reading One is a magazine article describing how gender affects language in the United States. Reading Two is an interview with a professor of communications focusing on gender-specific vocabulary.

The companion unit in *NorthStar: Listening and Speaking* deals with how regional and social dialects influence identity.

1 Focus on the Topic, PAGE 73

✪✪✪A PREDICTING

Suggested Time: 10 minutes ⏱

Focus
To get students thinking and talking about gender as they look at a picture of a baby and guess its sex; to predict the content of the unit based on the title and the photograph.

Setup
Ask students to look at the picture and write a description of it. Then ask them if they think the baby is a boy or girl and why.

Expansion/Homework
(1) If you have access to an overhead projector, you can use it to allow the whole class to view and discuss the photo together. (2) Ask students to exchange their writing to see if they share the same opinions.

✪✪B SHARING INFORMATION

Suggested Time: 15 minutes ⏱

Focus
To get students to share their experiences with gender-specific and nongender-specific items to bring personal experience to the topic of gender.

Setup
Have students read the instructions and fill in the chart. Help with vocabulary as needed. After students share their answers with a classmate, elicit answers from the class and list them on the board.

Expansion/Homework
(1) You might want to create a larger version of this chart to make into a transparency for the overhead projector, if available. Then you could note all students' responses in each box and discuss interesting anomalies. (2) Filling in the chart could be done as homework, with class time used for sharing answers.

✪✪✪ C **PREPARING TO READ**

BACKGROUND
Suggested Time: 20 minutes 🕐

Focus
To get students thinking about gender and sharing their experiences as they give their opinions on a variety of gender-related topics.

Setup
Have students complete the exercise individually before comparing their answers with a classmate (of a different cultural background, if possible). Then call on individual students to share their opinions with the class. Encourage disagreement as long as students' reasoning is sound.

Expansion/Homework
This exercise can be done as homework, with class time used for discussion.

Link to *NorthStar: Listening and Speaking*
Bring the issue of dialect into the discussion by adding the following questions to item 6: *Do you think that men and women speak different dialects? Do they use different words or grammatical forms? Do you think the way that men and women speak affects their identity?*

VOCABULARY FOR COMPREHENSION
Suggested Time: 15 minutes 🕐

Focus
To introduce the students to vocabulary that is typically used in discussions about gender; to aid their comprehension of Reading One.

Setup
Read the instructions and make sure that students understand that they must eliminate words that are not synonyms. Next, have them work individually without their dictionaries to guess the meanings of the words from context. Then they can compare their answers with a partner sitting nearby. Discuss the answers as a whole class and clarify any subtle differences in meaning between the correct answers (synonyms).

Expansion/Homework
(1) You could have the students complete the exercise in pairs to stimulate discussion of meaning. (2) This exercise could be assigned for homework.

❷ Focus on Reading, PAGE 76

✪✪✪ A   READING ONE: *Different Ways of Talking*
Suggested Time: 15 minutes 🕐

Focus
To get students motivated to read by asking them to predict the content of Reading One.

Setup
Have students read the first paragraph of Reading One and write their answers to the questions. Next, have them share their predictions in small groups before reading the article. When they finish reading, have them check their predictions again to see if they were correct. Then ask students to describe their accuracy with the predictions.

Expansion/Homework
(1) You might want to have the students discuss what the title means, asking them to give you examples of "different ways of talking." (2) The article could be read for homework, with class time used for checking predictions.

✪✪✪ READING FOR MAIN IDEAS
Suggested Time: 25 minutes 🕐

Focus
To get students to comprehend the global meaning of the text by distinguishing between correct main idea statements and false ones.

Setup
Have students scan the statements for any vocabulary they don't understand. Then have students work individually to identify the correct main ideas and rewrite the false ones. Elicit true/false answers and have students write corrected false statements on the board. Check for accuracy.

Expansion/Homework
(1) You might want to have students do this exercise as homework and then write the answers on the board in class. (2) Have students identify paragraphs where they found each main idea and where they found information to correct the false statements.

✪✪✪ READING FOR DETAILS
Suggested Time: 25 minutes 🕐

Focus
To get students to examine the text more thoroughly by choosing the correct detail from several choices and indicating where the detail was found.

Setup

Have students read the instructions and do the exercise individually. Next, have them work with partners sitting nearby to compare answers. Then go over the correct answers with the class.

Expansion/Homework

This exercise could be done as homework, with class time used to compare answers with partners.

✪✪ REACTING TO THE READING
Suggested Time: 25 minutes ⏱

Focus

To give students a chance to practice answering inference-level questions.

Setup

For Exercise 1, read the instructions and model item 1 with students, explaining how inference questions differ from literal ones. Have students work independently to answer the questions. Then have them compare answers in small groups (of different fluency levels), discussing any differences until they all agree. Encourage students to refer back to the text. Elicit answers and encourage students to support their answers by citing the paragraph and giving reasons. For Exercise 2, have students work in the same small groups before calling on individuals to share their ideas with the class.

Expansion/Homework

(1) Students could do Exercise 1 as homework. (2) You might want to have students order the multiple-choice answers in Exercise 1 according to which answer is most reasonable, less reasonable, and least reasonable. You could then elicit answers and encourage students to support their answers with reasons. (3) For more writing practice, you can assign Exercise 2 as homework and have students write one paragraph in response to each question. Then use class time for students to compare their answers in small groups.

✪✪✪ B   READING TWO: *Speaking of Gender*
Suggested Time: 30 minutes ⏱

Focus

To broaden the topic as students read an interview based on a professor's comments on gender and language.

Setup

Have students read the interview. In small groups (of different fluency levels), have students discuss their answers to the questions in Exercise 2. Elicit students' opinions, asking them to give support for their answers with reasons and explanations.

Expansion/Homework

(1) The reading could be done as homework, with class time used to discuss the questions. (2) For more writing practice, have students do item 1 in Exercise 2 as a written assignment at home or in class.

Link to *NorthStar: Listening and Speaking*

Select some vocabulary words from Unit 5 and have students use them in their discussion.

✪✪✪C **LINKING READINGS ONE AND TWO**

Suggested Time: 20 minutes 🕐

Focus

To get students to apply information from both readings to determine whether a male or female is speaking.

Setup

Read the instructions and have partners work in pairs (of mixed fluency levels) to complete the exercise. Then call on various pairs to share their answers with the class. Allow disagreement as long as students' reasoning is sound.

Expansion/Homework

(1) This exercise can be done as homework, with class time used for student explanation of their answers. (2) You could assign a quotation to each pair and have them become the "experts" on that quotation by finding information in the texts that indicates whether the speaker is male or female. (3) Have students write short dialogues using the same quotations and creating a context for a woman to say what a man typically says or for a man to say what a woman typically says.

❸ Focus on Vocabulary, PAGE 83

✪ EXERCISE 1

Suggested Time: 25 minutes 🕐

Focus

To help students focus on gender-specific words as well as words that can be considered unisex.

Setup

Read the instructions and have students complete the first part of the exercise with a partner (of a different fluency level). Next, go over the answers as a whole class. Then have students work with the same partner to do the second part of the exercise. Circulate among pairs and help with vocabulary as needed. Encourage students to include examples from their native languages.

Expansion/Homework

The first part of this exercise could be turned into a game. Divide the class into teams and set a time limit for the categorization task. Award a small prize to the team that is the first to complete the task correctly.

Link to *NorthStar: Listening and Speaking*

Review the concept of "stereotyping" by asking students to consider what stereotypes are associated with the words in this exercise. Have them discuss how stereotypes change with the use of unisex words.

✪ EXERCISE 2
Suggested Time: 15 minutes

Focus

To reinforce vocabulary from the unit and expand usage by having students use the vocabulary in a summary of Reading One.

Setup

Have students read the instructions and do the exercise. Elicit answers.

Expansion/Homework

(1) This exercise could be done as homework. (2) Correction could be done in class using a transparency of the exercise on the overhead projector.

✪ EXERCISE 3
Suggested Time: 25 minutes

Focus

To give students a chance to use new vocabulary in original expression as they review the content of Reading Two.

Setup

Read the instructions and make sure that students understand that they must use at least one vocabulary word in each question. Write an example question on the board. Next, have students write their questions individually before discussing them with partners sitting nearby. Circulate among pairs and listen for interesting questions to be shared with the whole class. Make sure that the vocabulary words are being used correctly.

Expansion/Homework

(1) This exercise can be done as homework, with class time used to share and answer questions. You might want to use student questions to create an error correction worksheet. (2) For more writing practice, students can expand their questions into written dialogues with Dr. Speakwell.

For extra vocabulary practice, have students work on the self-grading vocabulary activities for the unit on the NorthStar Companion Website at **http://www.longman.com/northstar**.

4 Focus on Writing, PAGE 85

✪✪✪ A STYLE: Comparing and Contrasting

Suggested Time: 25 minutes

Focus
To guide students as they use transitions of comparison and contrast to combine sentences.

Setup
Have students who are sitting next to each other work in pairs to read the paragraphs in Exercise 1 and discuss the meaning of the underlined words. Then have them read the explanation of transitions and complete Exercise 2. Ask different students to write their answers on the board. Other students can offer correction as needed. Answers may vary.

Expansion/Homework
(1) This exercise could be done as homework. (2) You might want to put Exercise 2 on a transparency for the overhead projector, if available, and correct it that way.

Link to *NorthStar: Listening and Speaking*
Have students use these transitions to write sentences comparing Peter's dialect to that of his American classmates. They can also use them to compare teenage speech to that of adults.

✪✪ B GRAMMAR: Using Modals for Requests

Suggested Time: 20 minutes

Focus
To practice using modals to make polite requests.

Setup
Have students look at the pairs of sentences and discuss the differences of meaning. Then have them read the explanation and do Exercises 2 and 3 individually before comparing their answers with those of a classmate sitting nearby. Next, have students write the answers for Exercise 3 on the board. Invite the students to do peer correction. Offer any further corrections as needed.

Expansion/Homework
(1) This exercise could be assigned as homework, with class time used for checking answers. (2) For more writing practice, you could have students write a letter to Deborah Tannen using modals to request more information about language and gender. (3) For further practice, offer exercises from *Focus on Grammar, Intermediate* and from *Fundamentals of English Grammar*. See the Grammar Book References on Student Book page 193 for specific units and chapters.

 For extra practice in the writing process, have students go to the *NorthStar Writing Activity Book, Intermediate*.

✪✪✪ C WRITING TOPICS

Focus
To integrate the vocabulary, concepts, grammar (using modals for requests), and style (comparing and contrasting) of the unit in a short writing assignment.

Setup
Assign this exercise for homework.

Expansion/Homework
Have partners read each other's drafts, checking for good paragraph development. Have the students mark paragraphs with TS if they find a topic sentence. Then have them look for supporting examples or details and mark them E1, E2, E3, and so on, and D1, D2, D3, and so on (for details that aren't examples). Next have them mark CS if they find a concluding sentence. When a student finishes marking the paper, you will need to check it. Then have the partners discuss their papers and revise any paragraphs that need more development.

Link to *NorthStar: Listening and Speaking*
Encourage students to use the vocabulary and grammar from Unit 5 in their writing.

✪ D RESEARCH TOPIC

Focus
To take students into the real world of TV programs to see how gender influences the language that is used.

Setup
Read the instructions and direct students to TV programs that they could watch. Go over the form and make sure that they understand each item. After the students complete their research, have them work in small groups (of students who work well together) to discuss similarities and write a summary. Encourage students to show videoclips while they present their findings to the class.

Expansion/Homework
You can allow students to use movies instead of TV programs.

Link to *NorthStar: Listening and Speaking*
Encourage students to use the vocabulary and grammar from Unit 5 as they write their summaries.

Ecotourism

OVERVIEW	
Theme:	Tourism
Readings:	*Tourists in a Fragile Land* 　　An opinion essay *A Travel Journal* 　　An account of a trip to Antarctica
Critical Thinking Skills:	Compare travel experiences Test assumptions about Antarctica Infer information not explicit in the text Analyze an author's argument Hypothesize another's point of view Compare and contrast points of view from two different texts Analyze relationships between words
Reading Tasks:	Make predictions Identify chronology in a text Read for details Paraphrase main ideas Relate texts to personal opinions Research ecotourism
Writing Tasks:	Write an opinion essay Analyze use of a thesis statement, supporting details, and 　　concluding statement in an essay Take notes in outline form Compose information questions Write a letter requesting information
Vocabulary:	Paraphrasing meaning Context clues Word associations Analogies Synonyms and antonyms
Grammar:	Past progressive and simple past

This unit deals with how tourism might endanger the remote and fragile environments of the earth. Reading One is an opinion essay about the dangers of allowing tourists to visit Antarctica. Reading Two is the diary of a tourist who enjoys her visit to Antarctica.

The companion unit in *NorthStar: Listening and Speaking* deals with the controversy related to tourism in Nai Soi, Thailand, where long-necked women display themselves to tourists for profit.

1 Focus on the Topic, PAGE 93

✪✪✪A   PREDICTING

Suggested Time: 10 minutes

Focus
To get students thinking about Antarctica to predict the content of the unit.

Setup
Look at the map and discuss the questions as a whole class. Ask students if they have ever visited these places or if they know anyone who has been there. As students discuss question 3, help with new vocabulary as needed.

Expansion/Homework
For more writing practice, you can have the students write answers to the questions and share them with a partner before discussing them as a whole class.

✪✪B   SHARING INFORMATION

Suggested Time: 20 minutes

Focus
To get students to talk about their past travel experiences with a focus on natural environments.

Setup
Go over the questions as a whole class before having students work in groups of four (of mixed cultural backgrounds, if possible) to answer them. Then call on each group to share their answers with the class.

Expansion/Homework
To stimulate discussion, you could bring in pictures of natural environments such as Hawaii, Alaska, and the Amazon.

✪✪✪ C ▐ PREPARING TO READ

BACKGROUND
Suggested Time: 15 minutes ⏱

Focus
To capture students' interest and get them thinking about Antarctica as they take a quiz on interesting facts about this continent.

Setup
Have students take the quiz. Explain that the purpose is not to test their knowledge but rather to get them thinking about information that will relate to the reading. In pairs (of different cultural backgrounds, if possible), have the students compare answers. Then go over the answers as a whole class, asking students if any answers surprised them.

Expansion/Homework
The quiz could be assigned as homework, with class time used to discuss answers.

VOCABULARY FOR COMPREHENSION
Suggested Time: 25 minutes ⏱

Focus
To introduce the vocabulary that students will encounter in Reading One to aid comprehension of the text.

Setup
Read the instructions and do the first example with the students to demonstrate the exercise. Ask students to complete the exercise individually, encouraging them to rely on context. Then elicit answers and discuss any items that were difficult.

Expansion/Homework
(1) This exercise could be assigned as homework. In class, elicit answers and explain the items as needed. (2) Ask students to quickly categorize the underlined words according to parts of speech.

2 Focus on Reading, PAGE 96

✪✪✪ A ▐ READING ONE: *Tourists in a Fragile Land*

Suggested Time: 10 minutes ⏱

Focus
To help students predict the content of the opinion essay.

Setup

Read and discuss the opinions as a whole class. Have students choose one individually. Then have students read the essay.

Expansion/Homework

(1) The reading could be done as homework. (2) You could ask students to keep their books closed while you write the title on the board. Have the students brainstorm opinions that might be expressed in the essay before checking the opinions in the book. Encourage students to consider all opinions as a possibility.

✪✪✪ READING FOR MAIN IDEAS
Suggested Time: 15 minutes ⏲

Focus

To confirm the predictions that students made in Section 2A; to review main ideas by placing them in order.

Setup

First, have students confirm their predictions and discuss which ones were correct. Then have them work individually to place the main ideas in order. Discuss the correct order as a whole class.

Expansion/Homework

This exercise could be assigned as homework.

✪✪✪ READING FOR DETAILS
Suggested Time: 30 minutes 🌐

Focus

To get students to examine the text more thoroughly by looking for details that can be used to complete an outline; to use details from the text to rewrite a series of false statements.

Setup

For Exercise 1, make sure that students understand that they must complete the outline with details that support the main ideas. Have them work in pairs (of mixed fluency levels) to complete the outline. Then go over the exercise as a whole class. For Exercise 2, read the instructions and discuss the example as a whole class. Have the students complete the exercise individually, and then have volunteers write their sentences on the board for peer correction and review.

Expansion/Homework

This could be done as homework. In class, have students compare answers with a classmate before reviewing them as a whole class.

✪✪ REACTING TO THE READING
Suggested Time: 25 minutes 🕑

Focus
To help students interpret and infer as they complete a series of statements; to give students a chance to empathize with the author and consider weaknesses in his arguments.

Setup
For Exercise 1, encourage students to select details that best fit their understanding of the text. Remind them of the importance of using details to make writing more interesting. For Exercise 2, divide the class into pairs (of mixed cultural backgrounds, if possible). After they have discussed the questions, call on pairs to share their answers with the class. List their answers to question 2 on the board and examine the weaknesses that students find in the essay.

Expansion/Homework
Exercise 1 could be assigned as homework, and Exercise 2 could be done in writing either in class or at home. Collect written responses to Exercise 2 and evaluate them for content.

Link to *NorthStar: Listening and Speaking*
Have students analyze weaknesses in the following argument: *Tourism to Nai Soi should stop because it is harmful to the local residents.*

✪✪✪ B   READING TWO: *A Travel Journal*
Suggested Time: 15 minutes 🕑

Focus
To help students consider another point of view by reading the journal of a tourist who enjoys Antarctica.

Setup
If possible, bring in a journal and ask students if they have ever kept one. Discuss why some people enjoy keeping journals when they travel. Have the students work in pairs (of mixed fluency levels) to discuss the questions. Then call on various pairs to share their answers with the class.

Expansion/Homework
The reading can be assigned as homework, with class time used to discuss the questions in Exercise 2.

Link to *NorthStar: Listening and Speaking*
Provide more writing practice by having students write a few excerpts of a travel journal based on an imagined visit to Nai Soi, Thailand.

✪✪✪ C **LINKING READINGS ONE AND TWO**

Suggested Time: 40 minutes 🕐

Focus

To get students to contrast the opinions expressed in both readings and to decide which opinion they agree with more.

Setup

Have students look at the chart and explain that they must complete it with information from both readings. Have them refer to the texts as they work individually. Then review the completed chart as a whole class, using an overhead transparency if possible. Next, have students write their answers for Exercise 2 individually. Call on a variety of students to share their answers with the class. Aim for a balance of opinions.

Expansion/Homework

(1) This section can be assigned as homework. (2) You might want to collect the written answers to Exercise 2 and respond to the content, evaluating how well students are able to give reasons to support their opinions. You can share outstanding examples with the whole class.

3 Focus on Vocabulary, PAGE 103

○ **EXERCISE 1**

Suggested Time: 15 minutes 🕐

Focus

To reinforce vocabulary studied in the unit as students do a word combination activity.

Setup

Read the instructions and example, and elicit a few combinations from the class. Then have the students work in pairs (of mixed fluency levels) to complete Exercise 1. Then call on various pairs to share their combinations with the class. List them on the board and explain why some combinations may not be correct.

Expansion/Homework

This activity can be done as homework.

Link to *NorthStar: Listening and Speaking*

Provide students with a few nouns and adjectives from Unit 6 and see how many combinations the students can create.

✪ EXERCISE 2
Suggested Time: 20 minutes

Focus

To extend and reinforce the meanings of the words in both readings through work with analogies.

Setup

Have students read the analogy types. Check their comprehension and discuss item 1. Then have the students complete the exercise individually and work with a partner sitting nearby to compare their answers. Next, call on individual students to share their analogies with the class. Offer correction as needed.

Expansion/Homework

This exercise works well as homework.

✪ EXERCISE 3
Suggested Time: 25 minutes

Focus

To give students a chance to use new vocabulary in a structured writing activity focusing on questions.

Setup

Read the instructions and discuss the example. Have the students work on this exercise in pairs (of mixed fluency levels). Then call on various pairs to share their questions with the class. Encourage a wide variety of questions and correct grammar as needed.

Expansion/Homework

(1) This activity could be done as homework. (2) You can play a Jeopardy-style game as a follow-up to this activity. Divide the class into teams and have them use vocabulary from the unit to create a set of answers and corresponding questions. Have them take turns reading statements to the class, and award points to teams that are able to ask questions that correspond to each statement.

 For extra vocabulary practice, have students work on the self-grading vocabulary activities for the unit on the NorthStar Companion Website at **http://www.longman.com/northstar**.

4 **Focus on Writing,** PAGE 105

✿✿✿A STYLE: Writing an Opinion Essay
Suggested Time: 30 minutes

Focus
To focus on the structure of an opinion essay and to give students a chance to complete an opinion essay with information from both readings.

Setup
Have students discuss the questions in Exercise 1. Then read the explanatory information in the chart and have students refer back to Reading One as they complete Exercise 2. Go over this activity as whole class. For Exercise 3, have students read the opinion essay and discuss the merits of the introduction and conclusion. Next, have them work individually to complete the essay with information from both readings. Then have them meet in small groups (of mixed fluency levels) to read their essays to each other.

Expansion/Homework
Assign Exercise 3 for homework. In class, collect student essays and evaluate them for content, focusing on how well the students are able to utilize information from the readings.

✿✿B GRAMMAR: Past Progressive and Simple Past
Suggested Time: 30 minutes

Focus
To familiarize students with the contrast between past progressive and simple past tense verbs.

Setup
Have students work in pairs (of varying fluency levels) to examine the example sentences in Exercise 1 and discuss differences between the underlined verbs in each sentence. Encourage students to share what they know about these forms. Then have them read the grammar explanations silently. Have students work independently to complete Exercise 2, and then have volunteers write their answers on the board for correction. After students complete Exercise 3, have them compare their sentences with a partner's. Different students can then write their sentences on the board and have their peers correct them. Offer correction when needed.

Expansion/Homework
(1) This entire activity works well as homework. You might want to have the students discuss the sentences in Exercise 1 with a partner before they do the homework. Then have them compare their answers for Exercises 2 and 3 in

the following class. Ask them to write their answers on the board for peer correction. (2) For further practice, offer exercises from *Focus on Grammar, Intermediate* and from *Fundamentals of English Grammar*. See the Grammar Book References on Student Book page 193 for specific units and chapters.

Link to *NorthStar: Listening and Speaking*
Have students write a brief description of an imagined visit to Nai Soi, Thailand, using *when* and *while*.

 For extra practice in the writing process, have students go to the *NorthStar Writing Activity Book, Intermediate*.

✪✪✪ C   WRITING TOPICS

Focus
To integrate the vocabulary, concepts, grammar (past progressive and simple past), and style focus (writing an opinion essay) of the unit in a short writing assignment.

Setup
Assign this exercise for homework, perhaps allowing several days.

Expansion/Homework
You could have the students exchange papers with a partner and look for two vocabulary words and two details that were used effectively.

Link to *NorthStar: Listening and Speaking*
Encourage students to use vocabulary from Unit 6 in their writing.

✪ D   RESEARCH TOPIC

Focus
To take students into the real world of ecotourism by having them research a fragile environment that attracts tourists.

Setup
Discuss the list of suggested travel destinations and brainstorm a few others. Then read through the research steps and ask students to think of a few other questions that can be added. Help students think of organizations they can write to for information. As they receive answers to their letters, ask students to share them with the class.

Expansion/Homework
(1) Students can also use the Internet to communicate with the organization of their choice. (2) You might want to post a few exemplary letters on a class bulletin board or web page. (3) Invite a member of a local environmental organization to visit your class. Ask the guest to answer the questions listed in this section and then have the students write a summary of the answers.

What's So Funny About That?

OVERVIEW

Theme:	Humor

Readings:	*The Story of* I Love Lucy
	    An autobiographical account
	Cosby: *A Different Kind of Family Show*
	    A TV show review

Critical Thinking Skills:	Interpret a photograph Explain the double meaning of a joke Analyze how humor reflects social and cultural values Compare and contrast characters, gender roles, and types of comedy Hypothesize another's point of view
Reading Tasks:	Make predictions Identify main ideas Locate information in a text Identify supporting details Recognize the organization of a text Compare and contrast information from two texts Research a comedy star
Writing Tasks:	Use parallel structure to combine sentences Write a TV show review using parallel structure Paraphrase a text Summarize the readings using new vocabulary Summarize a dialogue using noun clauses Write a biography of a comedy star
Vocabulary:	Context clues Word definitions Suffixes Word forms Vocabulary classification
Grammar:	Noun clauses with *wh-* words

UNIT SUMMARY

This unit explores American television comedy and how humor changes through the decades. Reading One is the autobiography of Lucille Ball. Reading Two is a critical review of *The Cosby Show*.

The companion unit in *NorthStar: Listening and Speaking* presents the issue of cross-cultural humor with a focus on American jokes.

1 Focus on the Topic, PAGE 113

✪✪✪ A PREDICTING

Suggested Time: 10 minutes

Focus
To get students thinking about the television show *I Love Lucy*.

Setup
Ask the students to look at the photo. Then have them work in pairs with a partner sitting nearby to write a caption for the photo. Call on pairs to share their captions with the class.

Expansion/Homework
This activity can be done as a whole class. Write two or three caption ideas on the board.

✪✪ B SHARING INFORMATION

Suggested Time: 15 minutes

Focus
To stimulate students' interest in the topic by presenting two types of jokes that are well known in American culture; to discuss students' own experience with jokes.

Setup
Ask individual students to read each explanation and example joke aloud. Ask them whether they understand the jokes, and clarify the ones that are unclear. Discuss whether or not people in their native cultures enjoy similar jokes. Then have students work in groups of four (of mixed cultural backgrounds, if possible) to answer and discuss the questions in Exercise 1 and 2. Call on each group to share interesting information with the class.

Expansion/Homework
The jokes can be read as homework and later discussed in class.

✪✪✪ C PREPARING TO READ

BACKGROUND
Suggested Time: 15 minutes 🕐

Focus
To familiarize students with the *I Love Lucy* show in preparation for Reading One.

Setup
Have students read the passage and mark their predictions. Work as a whole class to discuss what students expect to learn more about in Reading One. If possible, play a video clip from *I Love Lucy* to familiarize students with the show.

Expansion/Homework
This exercise can be assigned as individual homework. Have students discuss their predictions in class.

VOCABULARY FOR COMPREHENSION
Suggested Time: 20 minutes 🕐

Focus
To introduce vocabulary that students will need to discuss the topic of television comedy; to aid comprehension of Reading One.

Setup
Have students work individually to read the passage and choose the definition that best fits the meaning of the underlined words. Go over their choices, and explain new vocabulary as needed.

Expansion/Homework
You might want to read the vocabulary aloud to the class, teaching pronunciation and word form. Elicit the meaning from students, if possible. Then have students work in pairs to complete the exercise before you go over the answers as a whole class.

2 Focus on Reading, PAGE 117

✪✪✪ A READING ONE: *The Story of* I Love Lucy
Suggested Time: 5 minutes 🕐

Focus
To help students predict the content of the text by looking at a photo and guessing about the experiences that Lucille Ball and Desi Arnaz had while making the *I Love Lucy* show.

Setup

Have students discuss their ideas and affirm each one as a possibility. Ask them to explain why they gave each answer based on the photo. Write their ideas on the board.

Expansion/Homework

Have students vote on the best answer from those you wrote on the board. The reading can be assigned as homework. Have them confirm their predictions after they complete the reading.

✪✪✪ READING FOR MAIN IDEAS
Suggested Time: 15 minutes ⏲

Focus

To review main ideas by responding to a set of true/false statements; to rewrite false statements to make them true.

Setup

Have the students complete this exercise individually. Be sure to mention the importance of being able to locate information in a text, which this exercise requires them to do. Go over the answers as a whole class, making sure that the false statements have been rewritten correctly.

Expansion/Homework

This assignment can be done as homework.

Link to *NorthStar: Listening and Speaking*

Ask students to discuss whether the type of humor in *I Love Lucy* is known and appreciated in their home countries.

✪✪✪ READING FOR DETAILS
Suggested Time: 15 minutes ⏲

Focus

To show how main ideas are supported by details; to scan the text in order to eliminate details that are not included.

Setup

Students can complete this exercise in pairs (of mixed fluency levels). Make sure that students are able to locate the basis of their answers in the text.

Expansion/Homework

This exercise can be assigned as homework.

✪✪ REACTING TO THE READING
Suggested Time: 30 minutes ⏲

Focus

To confirm predictions made in Sections 1C and 2A; to help students distinguish between Lucille Ball the actress and Lucy Ricardo the character; to give students a chance to discuss important aspects of the show.

Setup

First, have students confirm their content predictions as indicated in Exercise 1. Then have them work in pairs (of mixed fluency levels) to complete Exercise 2. After checking this exercise as a whole class, have them write their answers to the questions in Exercise 3 before comparing them with their partner's. Call on individual students to share their answers with the class. Keep in mind that in some cultures, the roles of men and women may not have changed since the 1950s.

Expansion/Homework

For more writing practice, students can write stories based on the imagined experiences of either Lucille Ball or Lucy Ricardo. They can use the following opening lines to begin their stories: *(a) One day, Lucille Ball decided to make a major change in her show. (b) One day, Lucy Ricardo's dream of working in show business finally came true.*

✪✪✪ B   READING TWO: Cosby: *A Different Kind of Family Show*

Suggested Time: 20 minutes 🕐

Focus

To expand the topic of television comedy as students read a critical review of *The Cosby Show*.

Setup

If possible, bring in TV reviews from a newspaper to show the students. Have students read the article. Then give the students time in class to write their answers to the items in Exercise 2. Make sure that they base their responses on information from the text. When they are finished writing, have them meet in pairs (of mixed fluency levels) to share their answers. Call on several students to read their responses to the whole class; try to arrive at a consensus opinion based on information from the text.

Expansion/Homework

Exercise 2 can be done as homework. You might want to collect the written responses and evaluate the students' ability to base their answers on information from the text.

✪✪✪ C   LINKING READINGS ONE AND TWO

Suggested Time: 25 minutes 🕐

Focus

To make comparisons between the two television comedies; to imagine how Lucille Ball might have responded to *The Cosby Show*.

Setup

Have students write their responses to Exercise 1 individually. Then have them work in pairs (of mixed fluency levels) to share their answers. As you review their responses as a whole class, be sure to elicit specific examples of humor. Encourage the students to explain the types of humor that are most appreciated in their home cultures. For Exercise 2, read the introduction and incomplete article. Then have students work in pairs (of mixed fluency levels) to complete the article with information from both readings. Call on various pairs to share their completed articles with the class.

Expansion/Homework
This section could be assigned as homework.

Link to *NorthStar: Listening and Speaking*
Ask students to discuss how the humor of their home countries has changed through the decades.

3 Focus on Vocabulary, PAGE 126

✪ EXERCISE 1
Suggested Time: 15 minutes

Focus
To examine how suffixes are used to derive new word forms.

Setup
Read the explanation and have the students work individually to place words in appropriate categories. Then have them label each suffix with the word form from which it is derived. Review word forms as needed to make sure that students understand the concept.

Expansion/Homework
This exercise could be assigned as homework, with class time used to review word forms.

Link to *NorthStar: Listening and Speaking*
Have students use these suffixes to derive new word forms using the vocabulary from Unit 7.

✪ EXERCISE 2
Suggested Time: 25 minutes

Focus
To give students structured writing practice as they rewrite sentences using alternate word forms.

Setup
Go over the instructions and example, making sure that students understand what to do. Have them complete this exercise individually as you circulate and offer help as needed. If possible, use an overhead transparency to facilitate correction.

Expansion/Homework

(1) This exercise can be assigned as homework. (2) You could have students do this exercise in pairs (of mixed fluency levels). Assign one or two items to each pair, depending on class size. Have each pair write sentences on the board for peer review and correction.

✪ EXERCISE 3
Suggested Time: 30 minutes ⊚

Focus
To give students a chance to use the new vocabulary in original expression by writing a summary of what they have learned in the unit.

Setup
Work as a whole class to list ways in which American humor changed from the 1950s to the 1980s. Also, elicit a few different forms of the listed words. Then give students a chance to write their summaries in class. Collect them and evaluate how well students can use the new words in grammatical sentences.

Expansion/Homework
Students can write their summaries as homework. You can choose outstanding examples to share with the whole class and/or use student errors in word usage to create an error correction worksheet.

 For extra vocabulary practice, have students work on the self-grading vocabulary activities for the unit on the NorthStar Companion Website at **http://www.longman.com/northstar**.

4 Focus on Writing, PAGE 128

✪✪✪ A   STYLE: Parallel Structure
Suggested Time: 25 minutes ⊚

Focus
To make students aware of parallel structure and give them practice using it in their own writing.

Setup
Have the students read the example sentences and label the subjects and verbs. Then ask students to go over the information in the chart before completing Exercise 2 individually. Have volunteers write their sentences on the board for review and correction. Next, encourage them to use vocabulary from the unit in

Exercise 3. Have the students share their completed paragraphs with a partner sitting nearby. Then call on individuals to read their paragraphs to the class.

Expansion/Homework

(1) This section can be assigned as homework. (2) For more writing practice, ask students to write paragraphs using parallel structure to describe other forms of humor (humorous people, humorous cartoon strips, etc.).

Link to *NorthStar: Listening and Speaking*

Have students use parallel structure in describing the humor of a famous comedian in their home cultures. Encourage them to use vocabulary from Unit 7 in their writing.

✪✪ B | GRAMMAR: Noun Clauses with *Wh-* words

Suggested Time: 30 minutes

Focus

To use noun clauses to write about television comedies.

Setup

Have students work in pairs to read the paragraph and identify the underlined phrases. Encourage them to share what they already know about these forms. Then have them label the next set of sentences as directed. Read the explanatory chart and have students examine and explain the examples that follow. Then have them work in pairs (of mixed fluency levels) to read the dialogue and complete the sentences in Exercise 2. Next, have them work with the same partner to complete Exercise 3. Call on various pairs to share their answers with the class. Make sure that several examples are given for each item, and offer more explanation and examples as needed.

Expansion/Homework

(1) You may want to assign this section as homework, with class time used for correction and review. (2) For further practice, offer exercises from *Focus on Grammar, Intermediate* and from *Fundamentals of English Grammar*. See the Grammar Book References on Student Book page 193 for specific units and chapters.

Link to *NorthStar: Listening and Speaking*

Have students use noun clauses to write explanations of the jokes presented in Unit 7. (Example: The pun in Section 1C can be explained as follows: The first person asks, "How do you make friends with a squirrel? The second person says that you have to climb a tree and act like a nut. This joke is funny if you know what *nut* means. The first meaning is "what squirrels eat for food" and the second meaning is "how we describe a crazy person.")

 For extra practice in the writing process, have students go to the *NorthStar Writing Activity Book, Intermediate*.

✪✪✪ C WRITING TOPICS

Focus
To integrate the vocabulary, concepts, grammar (noun clauses with *wh-* words), and style focus (parallel structure) of the unit in a short writing assignment.

Setup
Assign this exercise for homework, allowing students adequate time to complete the task.

Expansion/Homework
Use samples of student writing to review parallel structure. Create an error correction exercise from sentences in which students attempted to use parallel structure but did so incorrectly or incompletely.

✪ D RESEARCH TOPIC

Focus
To help students explore the real world of comedy by having them write reports on a comedy star of their choice.

Setup
Read the listed choices and elicit other comedians that students enjoy. Go over the questions that students need to answer as they write biographies of the stars. Then have students meet in small groups (of mixed cultural backgrounds, if possible) to share their reports with each other. Have each group select the most interesting report to be presented to the whole class.

Expansion/Homework
(1) If time allows, you can have individual students present their reports to the whole class. (2) You might want to post outstanding reports on the class bulletin board or webpage. (3) If students have access to PowerPoint technology, they can use it to enhance their reports.

Always in Fashion

OVERVIEW	
Theme:	Fashion

Readings:	*The Search for Beauty*
	    A passage on plastic surgery
	My Wife Wants to Look Younger
	    An excerpt from a journal

Critical Thinking Skills:	Compare assumptions and values about beauty Draw conclusions Interpret word usage Infer information not explicit in the text Hypothesize another's point of view Synthesize information from two texts Make recommendations using information from the texts Analyze cause and effect Analyze trends in fashion
Reading Tasks:	Make predictions Interpret a timeline Locate main ideas in the text Read for details Connect texts to personal interests, experiences, and values
Writing Tasks:	Write opinion statements using new vocabulary Write a persuasive letter Use transitions to show cause and effect Write a narrative in the past Summarize an interview in a paragraph Write a passage using the past tenses Report research findings on department store merchandise
Vocabulary:	Word definitions Word association
Grammar:	Describing the past with *used to*

UNIT SUMMARY

The topic of this unit is cosmetic surgery, one recent way in which people have tried to improve their looks. Reading One is an article on the history of fashion in the West, with a focus on cosmetic surgery. Reading Two is an excerpt from the diary of a man whose wife is having a facelift.

The companion unit in *NorthStar: Listening and Speaking* deals with changing attitudes toward traditional and casual dress.

1 Focus on the Topic, PAGE 135

✪✪✪A PREDICTING

Suggested Time: 10 minutes

Focus
To get students thinking about cosmetic surgery as they respond to an ad that promotes cosmetic surgery as a means of becoming more beautiful.

Setup
Ask students to describe the people in the ad; ask if they think they are good-looking. Make sure that they understand the term *cosmetic surgery*. Read through the questions together, checking student comprehension, and then give students five minutes to write their responses. You might have pairs exchange their writing.

Expansion/Homework
Instead of sharing their responses with a partner, individual students can read their responses to the whole class.

✪✪B SHARING INFORMATION

Suggested Time: 20 minutes

Focus
To give students an opportunity to reflect on their own attitudes toward fashion and beauty; to compare their attitudes with those of other students.

Setup
Read the instructions and make sure that students understand the difference between "strongly agree" and "strongly disagree." It is also helpful to read the survey items as a whole class to make sure that students understand each one. After completing the survey, have students compare their answers in small groups (of mixed cultural backgrounds, if possible). Encourage students to explain their views and why they may disagree with the views of others.

Expansion/Homework

After students have compared their responses in small groups, you might want to have them choose one or two items that elicited the most disagreement and report them to the class. It might also be interesting to see if there are any patterns of similarity among the members of the class.

✪✪✪ C PREPARING TO READ

BACKGROUND
Suggested Time: 15 minutes

Focus

To raise students' consciousness of the connection between changing times and the ways in which people try to improve their looks; to begin thinking critically about cosmetic surgery.

Setup

If possible, show students a picture of a 1920s flapper. Explain that the beauty ideal of that decade was slenderness, much as it is today. Elicit students' background knowledge of 1950s fashion, perhaps by mentioning Marilyn Monroe as an example of a beautiful woman who used makeup and hair color. In discussing the 1980s, ask the students if they know of a cosmetic surgery technique (liposuction) that people started to use to change the shape of their bodies. Then call on individual students to answer the questions.

Expansion/Homework

(1) You can have the students discuss the questions in pairs before sharing their answers. (2) For more writing practice, have the students choose a discussion question and write a paragraph in response to it. (3) You may also want to have the students predict the concept of "beauty" for the year 2010.

VOCABULARY FOR COMPREHENSION
Suggested Time: 15 minutes

Focus

To familiarize students with vocabulary that is frequently used to describe fashion; to prepare students for comprehension of Reading One.

Setup

Read the target words aloud and model their pronunciation. Go over the definitions, and offer explanations and examples as needed. Complete the cloze passage as a class, paying close attention to the form of target words and how they fit the context of each sentence.

Expansion/Homework

This activity could be done individually, either as homework or as a self-test.

Link to *NorthStar: Listening and Speaking*

The second paragraph of the cloze passage is related to Listening One, which focuses on traditional clothing. This might stimulate a discussion of traditional versus modern clothing. Encourage students to discuss which style they think is more beautiful.

2 Focus on Reading, PAGE 138

✪✪✪ A   READING ONE: *The Search for Beauty*

Suggested Time: 15 minutes ⏱

Focus

To give students an opportunity to link their personal knowledge to a central theme of the text: while fashions change, the desire for beauty remains the same.

Setup

Read the first paragraph aloud, then direct students to complete the writing assignment individually. Give them approximately five minutes to write their responses in the space provided. Call on individual students (or ask for volunteers) to share their writing with the class.

Expansion/Homework

Students can read what they have written to a partner. You might want to circulate among pairs and find students who have done a particularly good job of addressing the questions. These responses can then be shared with the whole class. The reading can be assigned as homework.

✪✪✪ READING FOR MAIN IDEAS

Suggested Time: 15 minutes ⏱

Focus

To locate main ideas in the text and to give students practice working with paraphrased information.

Setup

Explain to the students that the sentences are paraphrases of main ideas. When students locate them in the text, ask them to underline them. You might want to explain that underlining is a valuable study skill that will help them in the future as they read longer texts and need to keep track of main ideas.

Expansion/Homework

This exercise would work well as homework, with class time used to check answers.

✪✪✪ READING FOR DETAILS
Suggested Time: 15–20 minutes

Focus

To reread the text carefully in order to determine whether statements are true or false; to rewrite false statements by changing details to make them true.

Setup

Have students read the statements individually, checking true or false based on their memory of Reading One. Next, ask them to check the text to confirm true answers and rewrite false ones. Go over the answers as a whole class.

Expansion/Homework

Ask students (who are sitting next to each other) to work in pairs to compare their answers and discuss any differences. Students who finish early can work in pairs to create true/false statements of their own to be exchanged with their classmates.

✪✪ REACTING TO THE READING
Suggested Time: 25 minutes

Focus

To help students think creatively about the information in the text and to draw inferences.

Setup

For Exercise 1, explain to students that they need to use their imaginations and make a good guess based on what they have read. You may need to ask some leading questions to get them started, for example, *Why do you think American women admired French fashions in the 1800s? Do you think these fashions were beautiful?* Have the students work in small groups (of different cultural backgrounds, if possible) to complete the sentences. Encourage a variety of ideas. For Exercise 2, have students write their answers individually and discuss their answers with a classmate (of a different cultural background, if possible). Then call on a few individual students to share their ideas with the class.

Expansion/Homework

(**1**) You could give each group the task of focusing on one item in Exercise 1 and coming up with two or three possibilities that could then be discussed by the whole class. (**2**) Exercise 2 can be assigned as homework, with class time used for sharing responses.

Link to *NorthStar: Listening and Speaking*

Provide more writing practice by asking students to write a paragraph describing the period(s) of history when traditional clothing was commonly worn in their home cultures.

✪✪✪ B ▐ **READING TWO:** *My Wife Wants to Look Younger*

Suggested Time: 30 minutes 🕐

Focus
To add a male perspective to the topic of fashion by having students read the diary of a man whose wife undergoes cosmetic surgery.

Setup
If possible, bring in a diary or journal and show it to the class. Ask if any students have ever kept a diary. Then read through each entry as a class, asking different students to read each entry aloud. Allow time to discuss student questions and reactions. Then have students discuss the questions in Exercise 2 in small groups (male and female, if possible). As a follow-up, have students write their own diary entries in Exercise 3 and share them with a partner sitting nearby.

Expansion/Homework
(1) Some of the discussion questions in Exercise 2 could be assigned as writing topics for homework. (2) For more writing practice, the diary-writing activity in Exercise 3 could be expanded to several paragraphs.

✪✪✪ C ▐ **LINKING READINGS ONE AND TWO**

Suggested Time: 20 minutes 🕐

Focus
To apply information from Reading One to solving the problems of people who want to improve their looks. (Some problems will require the application of information from Reading Two; for example, the "older sister" in item 2 could possibly have a facelift.)

Setup
If possible, bring in a picture of a very unattractive person and ask the students to discuss how cosmetic surgery could be used to help the person look better. Then read the instructions and have students work in pairs (of mixed fluency levels) to write sentences. Encourage them to use modals of possibility; for example, in item 1: *He might use cosmetic surgery to make his hair grow back. The surgeon could plant new hair on his bald spot.* Ask the students to write complete sentences, and make sure that they refer to both readings. Then have various students write their sentences on the board for peer correction.

Expansion/Homework
(1) This exercise could be done individually as homework. (2) One item could be assigned to each pair, who would report their answers back to the class. (3) Ask students to create a matching exercise once they have written their sentences; they can exchange sentences with another pair, who will try to match the sentence to the appropriate item. (Example: "The doctor could perform liposuction" can be matched with item 3.) (4) After the students have completed their sentences and received feedback, have them decide whether they would advise cosmetic surgery in each case.

❸ Focus on Vocabulary, PAGE 146

✪ EXERCISE 1
Suggested Time: 15 minutes ⏲

Focus
To focus on adjectives from the unit and how they can be used in combination with various nouns.

Setup
Read the instructions and discuss the example, asking students to explain their own concepts of the "ideal man" or the "ideal personality." Then have them work in groups of two or three to complete the exercise. Encourage discussion and experimentation. Point out that some words, such as *popular*, are used quite widely, while others, such as *slim*, are used in a very limited way.

Expansion/Homework
You can help students develop more vocabulary knowledge by having them go to the board in small groups and work within a time limit to list words and phrases that they associate with one of the items. For example, students may list such words as *marriage, friendship, parenthood, true love,* and *citizenship* in association with the item "permanent relationship."

✪ EXERCISE 2
Suggested Time: 25 minutes ⏲

Focus
To provide the students with guided writing practice and to reinforce the use of the vocabulary of the unit.

Setup
Look at the example sentence and ask students to use it as a model for their own sentences. (Call on two or three students for examples.) Once they understand that they need to use the same structure but create a new sentence using the target word, have them work on this exercise individually. Then call on volunteers to write their sentences on the board for peer correction.

Expansion/Homework
This exercise can be assigned as homework, with class time used for correction. You may want to collect the sentences and use them to create an error correction worksheet.

✪ EXERCISE 3
Suggested Time: 30 minutes ⏲

Focus
To give the students a chance to use new vocabulary in original expression; to help students use what they have learned from the readings to write a letter.

Setup

Read the instructions and remind the students that they need to use at least five of the target words. Review letter-writing format as needed. Give the students time to write in class, and offer individual help as needed. Then have students exchange their letters with a partner nearby before collecting them all for individual correction.

Expansion/Homework

You can assign this exercise as homework. Use errors to create an error correction worksheet. Also, use well-written sentences as an example of correct word usage for the whole class to review.

 For extra vocabulary practice, have students work on the self-grading vocabulary activities for the unit on the NorthStar Companion Website at **http://www.longman.com/northstar**.

4 Focus on Writing, PAGE 147

✪✪✪A STYLE: Cause and Effect

Suggested Time: 30 minutes

Focus

To help students use transitions of cause and effect in writing; to practice combining independent clauses as well as writing complex sentences.

Setup

Have students look at the example sentences and discuss the meaning of underlined words. Read the explanation of transitions used to show cause and effect. Explain that effective writers are able to use a variety of transition words to combine ideas. Then have the students complete Exercise 2 individually. Remind them to refer to the examples for appropriate comma use. Go over the answers as a whole class. For Exercise 3, have students refer to Reading Two to write five sentences using transitions of cause and effect. Make sure that they use a variety of transitions in their writing. Then have volunteers write their sentences on the board for peer correction.

Expansion/Homework

Exercises 2 and 3 can be assigned as homework.

Link to *NorthStar: Listening and Speaking*

Provide more writing practice by having students write about the use of casual clothing in the workplace using transitions of cause and effect.

✪✪B   GRAMMAR: Describing the Past with *Used to*

Suggested Time: 30 minutes

Focus

To describe fashion-related habits in the past using the form *used to*.

Setup

For Exercise 1, have students examine the passage from Reading One and note the form *used to*. Elicit their knowledge of this form's meaning before having them read the grammar chart. Then go on to Exercise 2, which is a quick warm-up intended to prepare students for the more challenging tasks of Exercises 3 and 4. Complete Exercise 2 as a whole class and have students do Exercise 3 individually. Call on individual students to read their paragraphs aloud to the class. Then have students complete their interviews (Exercise 4) with a partner (from a different cultural background, if possible). Next, collect the resulting paragraphs and share outstanding examples with the class. You may want to create an error correction exercise from their paragraphs, focusing on the misuse of *used to*.

Expansion/Homework

(1) You can bring in pictures of traditional American dress (cowboys, Pilgrims, etc.) and have students write descriptions using the *used to* form. **(2)** Students can also write about beauty rituals (e.g., hairdressing, makeup application) performed in the past. **(3)** For further practice, offer exercises from *Focus on Grammar, Intermediate* and from *Fundamentals of English Grammar*. See the Grammar Book References on Student Book page 193 for specific units and chapters.

 For extra practice in the writing process, have students go to the *NorthStar Writing Activity Book, Intermediate*.

✪✪✪C   WRITING TOPICS

Focus

To integrate the vocabulary, concepts, grammar (the past with *used to*) and style focus (cause and effect) of the unit in a short writing assignment.

Setup

Assign this writing as homework, allowing adequate time for students to complete the task.

Expansion/Homework

(1) Use samples of student writing to model good work. Choose two or three samples that reflect effective use of the grammar and style from the unit. **(2)** You could also discuss the process-writing steps of first draft, editing, proofreading, and final draft.

Link to *NorthStar: Listening and Speaking*

Encourage students to use vocabulary from Unit 8 in their writing.

✪D RESEARCH TOPIC

Focus
To give students a chance to apply what they have learned as they explore the real world of department-store fashion.

Setup
Identify local department stores that students can visit. Group students according to the aspect of fashion they would like to examine. Have them write up their findings and exchange their reports with other groups. Guide a whole-class discussion by asking students to comment on what they found most interesting in the reports.

Expansion/Homework
(1) Allow students to use online shopping catalogs as an alternative. (2) As a follow-up to the reporting activity, ask students to respond to the following questions: *Do you think that fashion can be used instead of cosmetic surgery to make people more attractive? What kinds of colors make people more beautiful? What kinds of styles make people look younger and slimmer?*

Link to *NorthStar: Listening and Speaking*
Ask students to look for ways in which traditional clothing has been incorporated into current fashion styles (e.g., nightgowns patterned after the traditional Japanese kimono; Western cowboy boots worn as a fashion style).

Crime and Punishment

OVERVIEW

Theme:	Punishment

Readings:	*Life in Prison Is Still Life: Why Should a Killer Live?*
	Why Do We Kill People to Show That Killing People Is Wrong?
	    Two newspaper op-ed articles
	Graphs
	    Statistics on the death penalty

Critical Thinking Skills:	Distinguish arguments for and against capital punishment
	Compare and contrast punishment practices in different
	    cultures
	Identify an author's point of view
	Hypothesize an author's values based on information in
	    the text
	Interpret bar graphs and a pie chart
	Draw conclusions
	Correlate examples with abstractions

Reading Tasks:	Make predictions Identify supporting ideas in an argument Relate supporting details to main ideas Identify contrasting arguments Research a country's use of capital punishment
Writing Tasks:	Support opinions with facts and data Write an opinion paragraph using new vocabulary Compose complex and compound sentences Edit a passage to vary sentence structure Write a letter to the editor Write a report on research
Vocabulary:	Context clues Word definitions Abstract nouns Appropriate word usage
Grammar:	Contrast: present perfect and present perfect progressive

---

UNIT SUMMARY

This unit focuses on the capital punishment debate. Reading One is a set of two editorials: one in favor of capital punishment and one against it. Reading Two is a set of graphs presenting information on the death penalty.

The companion unit in *NorthStar: Listening and Speaking* deals with the legal and social aspects of corporal punishment of children by parents.

1 Focus on the Topic, PAGE 155

✪✪✪ A PREDICTING

Suggested Time: 10–15 minutes ⏲

Focus
To get students thinking about capital punishment by asking them to react to a photo of a pro–capital punishment demonstration. *Note:* Some students may not understand the information on the signs in the photograph. Encourage them to describe what people are doing, and help them understand what is happening in the photo.

Setup
Read the questions and have students write short answers before sharing their ideas with a partner sitting nearby. Circulate among pairs, encouraging students who understand the concept of capital punishment to explain it to their classmates. Check to make sure the entire class understands what capital punishment is. This will help students choose words they think are related. Ask students to choose any words from the list that they think relate to the photo and explain their choices. Encourage a wide range of answers and provide vocabulary as needed.

Expansion/Homework
For more writing practice, have students write sentences using the words they chose to describe the photo. (Example: Capital punishment is used to punish *crime*.)

✪✪ B SHARING INFORMATION

Suggested Time: 15 minutes ⏲

Focus
To elicit students' background knowledge of capital punishment.

Setup
Read the questions together, and then divide students into small groups (of different cultural backgrounds, if possible). To facilitate cooperative learning, appoint a discussion leader and information-recorder for each group. Circulate among the groups, and provide vocabulary as needed. List the groups' answers

to items 1 and 2 on the chalkboard or transparency. Be sensitive to students' attitudes; some may feel embarrassed about their governments' policies, so be careful not to focus on a particular country unless the student seems willing to volunteer information.

Expansion/Homework
To help students discuss item 3, it might be helpful to draw a T-chart on the chalkboard or on a transparency to help them organize their ideas. One side of the chart can be used to list ideas under the rubric "fair," while the other side can be used to list ideas under the rubric "unfair."

✪✪✪C PREPARING TO READ

BACKGROUND
Suggested Time: 20 minutes 🕐

Focus
To prepare students for Reading One by having them think specifically about prison life.

Setup
Explain to students that they must first choose two cultures with which they are familiar. Explain unknown vocabulary items as needed. This exercise lends itself well to a survey, which can be done by keeping a tally of all the answers. Look for patterns: Are there any similarities or differences across cultures?

Expansion/Homework
You may want to have students use the information from this chart to write a paragraph about prison life in a particular culture.

VOCABULARY FOR COMPREHENSION
Suggested Time: 10 minutes 🕐

Focus
To familiarize students with vocabulary that is typically found in readings on crime and punishment; to aid comprehension of Reading One.

Setup
Call on volunteers to read the sentences aloud, and help with the pronunciation of underlined words. Students can then work individually to match vocabulary with definitions. Encourage students to use context clues. Go over the answers as a whole class.

Expansion/Homework
This exercise would work well as a homework assignment. When you review it in class, be sure to model pronunciation and offer further explanations of meaning as needed.

2 Focus on Reading, PAGE 158

✪✪✪ A READING ONE: *Two Points of View*

Suggested Time: 15 minutes ⏰

Focus
To give students an opportunity to explore opinions for and against capital punishment in the context of newspaper editorials.

Setup
You might want to bring in a newspaper and show students the editorial section. Next, read the two headlines as a class and identify them as either pro or con. Discuss at least one idea associated with each opinion before having students write. Then discuss students' expectations as a whole class. If possible, give students time in class to read the editorials.

Expansion/Homework
You might want to have students work in pairs to write down ideas associated with the headlines. Refer students to the list of words in Section 1A on page 155 and encourage them to use this vocabulary in their lists.

✪✪✪ READING FOR MAIN IDEAS
Suggested Time: 15 minutes ⏰

Focus
To have students match main ideas to the pro and con opinions that they support.

Setup
First, have students review the positions of Opinion A and Opinion B in the editorials. Then have students work individually to match the main ideas to Opinion A or Opinion B based on information from the text. As they finish, pair students (who are sitting next to each other) to compare answers. If they disagree, ask them to check the texts again carefully. Go over the answers as a whole class.

Expansion/Homework
This exercise could be done as homework.

✪✪✪ READING FOR DETAILS
Suggested Time: 15 minutes ⏰

Focus
To help students relate details to main ideas by having them match details to the main ideas they worked with in the previous section.

Setup
Once you are sure that students understand the example, have them work on this exercise individually. They must understand that each detail offers specific information that relates to one of the more general main ideas. Then they can refer back to the text. If students are having difficulty, complete the exercise as a class.

Expansion/Homework

You could ask students to think of other details that are related to the main ideas. For example, Main Idea 8 states that "Prison can sometimes improve a person." Students might be able to think of some examples to support this idea: One prisoner learns to read, another gets a GED (General Education Diploma), and yet another takes college courses.

✪✪ REACTING TO THE READING
Suggested Time: 25 minutes ⏲

Focus

To confirm predictions made earlier about the text; to draw inferences about the writers' attitudes and beliefs based on the opinions they have expressed.

Setup

First, have the students discuss the accuracy of their predictions about the articles. Next, explain that editorial writing often reveals the attitudes and beliefs of the writer. Before they look at the items in Exercises 2 and 3, ask students to imagine what kind of person wrote each of the editorials in Reading One. Then ask them to work in pairs (of mixed fluency levels) to select qualities that correspond to each writer. Make sure they can support their choices with information from the text. For Exercise 4, read the instructions and have the students complete the chart in small groups (of mixed fluency levels). Next, have them write their opinions on capital punishment individually. Explain that they must state whether or not they agree with it and give reasons for their opinion. Then call on individual students to share their opinions with the class; aim for a balance of pro and con opinions.

Expansion/Homework

(1) To promote more discussion, have the students complete Exercises 2 and 3 in small groups (of different cultural backgrounds, if possible). (2) In Exercise 4, you might want to collect the students' writing in order to give individual feedback; focus on their use of support for their opinions.

Link to *NorthStar: Listening and Speaking*

Have students make inferences about the parents and experts who spoke in Listening One. Ask students to consider the following questions: *What does a parent who supports spanking believe about children? What does a parent who opposes spanking believe about children? What kind of person chooses to become an expert on raising children?* Encourage students to focus on attitudes and beliefs in their answers.

✪✪✪ B   READING TWO: *Graphs*
Suggested Time: 25 minutes ⏲

Focus

To extend the topic of capital punishment as students read and interpret a variety of graphs.

Setup

As a warm-up, you might want to bring in charts and graphs from newspapers and magazines to show the class. Explain that charts and graphs are used in the popular media and in academic texts as a concise way of presenting information. Then read the introduction and make sure students understand what to read in each graph. Next, pair them with a classmate (of a different fluency level) to read and interpret the graphs. Circulate among pairs and offer help as they work on the questions. Then go over the answers as a whole class.

Expansion/Homework

This reading could be assigned as homework, with class time used to review answers.

✪✪✪ C **LINKING READINGS ONE AND TWO**

Suggested Time: 15 minutes 🕐

Focus

To give students a chance to apply information from Reading Two to a set of excerpts from Reading One as they practice supporting arguments with data.

Setup

Explain the importance of using facts and data to support opinions in writing. Then read the instructions and have the students complete the exercise in pairs (of mixed fluency levels). Circulate among pairs and offer help as needed; if necessary, you can direct them to the appropriate graphs, but make sure they locate the needed information on their own. Call on several pairs to share their answers with the class. Encourage a wide variety of responses.

Expansion/Homework

This exercise can be assigned as homework.

Link to *NorthStar: Listening and Speaking*

Challenge students to use the library or Internet to find facts and data on corporal punishment. Have them bring this information to class and use it to support arguments for and against the spanking of children by parents.

🔳 Focus on Vocabulary, PAGE 165

✪ **EXERCISES 1 AND 2**

Suggested Time: 20 minutes 🕐

Focus

To make students aware of abstract nouns; to examine abstract nouns that are commonly used to discuss the topic of capital punishment.

Setup

Read the instructions and elicit more examples of abstract nouns. Then have students complete Exercises 1 and 2 individually before comparing answers with a partner sitting nearby.

Expansion/Homework

(1) Exercise 2 can be done as homework. (2) For more writing practice, you can ask students to choose five of the abstract nouns from Exercise 2 and use each one in an original sentence.

Link to *NorthStar: Listening and Speaking*

Have students review the new vocabulary items in Unit 9 and identify any abstract nouns.

✪ EXERCISE 3
Suggested Time: 15 minutes 🕐

Focus

To increase students' awareness of word choices and how different words have different degrees or shades of meaning.

Setup

You might want to do the first two items as a class to make sure that students understand the task. Then have them complete the exercise individually. As you review the answers as a whole class, encourage students to ask questions about the differences in meaning that result when different word choices are made.

Expansion/Homework

To give the students more opportunities to work with synonyms, have them work in pairs to generate lists of synonyms for each underlined word in the exercise. For example, in item 7 they might think of *damage, harm, ruin* as synonyms for *hurt*. Discuss the differences in meaning that occur when synonyms are used.

✪ EXERCISE 4
Suggested Time: 25 minutes 🕐

Focus

To give students a chance to use new vocabulary in original expression as they explore the idea of punishment in the future.

Setup

Make sure that students understand the writing prompt. Give them ample time to write in class, and offer individual help as needed. Collect the paragraphs and correct errors in word usage.

Expansion/Homework

(1) This exercise can be done as homework. (2) You can share exemplary responses with the whole class and/or create an error correction worksheet focusing on word usage.

 For extra vocabulary practice, have students work on the self-grading vocabulary activities for the unit on the NorthStar Companion Website at **http://www.longman.com/northstar**.

4 Focus on Writing, PAGE 168

✪✪✪ A STYLE: Sentence Variety

Suggested Time: 25–30 minutes

Focus

To introduce students to the concept of sentence variety by giving them practice in writing simple, compound, and complex sentences.

Setup

Read and discuss the passage in Exercise 1. Then read the chart, making sure that students understand the importance of sentence variety as a writing technique. As students combine sentences in Exercise 2, have them refer to the explanation chart and make sure they use correct punctuation and capitalization. Read the letter in Exercise 3 as a whole class and clarify the task as needed. You may want to model one or two changes with the class.

Expansion/Homework

Exercises 2 and 3 could be assigned as homework.

✪✪ B GRAMMAR: Contrast—Present Perfect and Present Perfect Progressive

Suggested Time: 20 minutes

Focus

To contrast the two verb tenses, present perfect and present perfect progressive, in the context of a prisoner's story.

Setup

Read the two paragraphs and have students discuss the two verb tenses. As the students work individually on Exercise 2, have them refer to the grammar chart and look at the verbs in parentheses to determine whether they are verbs of action or emotion. Go over the answers and offer more explanation of the verb tenses as needed.

Expansion/Homework

(1) This exercise can be done as homework, with class time used for explanation and correction. (2) For more writing practice, you may want to have the

students write a paragraph describing a recent criminal case using the two tenses. To generate ideas, have students check their local newspaper. (3) For further practice, offer exercises from *Focus on Grammar, Intermediate* and from *Fundamentals of English Grammar*. See the Grammar Book References on Student Book page 193 for specific units and chapters.

 For extra practice in the writing process, have students go to the *NorthStar Writing Activity Book, Intermediate*.

✪✪✪ C WRITING TOPICS

Focus
To integrate the vocabulary, concepts, grammar (present perfect and present perfect progressive), and style focus (sentence variety) of the unit in a short writing assignment.

Setup
Assign this exercise as homework, perhaps allowing several days.

Expansion/Homework
Use samples from student writing to reinforce the concept of sentence variety.

Link to *NorthStar: Listening and Speaking*
Encourage students to use vocabulary from Unit 9 in their writing.

✪ D RESEARCH TOPICS

Focus
To give students a chance to learn more about a specific country and its laws relating to the death penalty.

Setup
If possible, bring in a map of the world and ask students to name countries that administer or do not administer the death penalty. Encourage guessing. Next, read the instructions and the list of suggested countries. Then read the research steps and questions, making sure that students understand the process. Brainstorm other questions that can be added to the list. After students have completed their research, place them in small groups (of students who work well together) to share information and write a report. Appoint a spokesperson for each group to read the group's report to the class.

Expansion/Homework
(1) If students have access to PowerPoint technology, they can use it to enhance their reports. (2) You might consider having the students create posters summarizing their findings to be placed on the classroom wall. (3) If you are working with another teacher, you might be able to arrange for your students to visit his or her class and present a panel discussion on their findings.

Finding a Spouse

OVERVIEW	
Theme:	Marriage

Readings:	*Finding a Spouse*
	    An anthropological article
	What's Wrong with Tradition?
	    A letter to the editor

Critical Thinking Skills:	Identify personal assumptions about marriage Classify information Identify underlying cultural values Evaluate information in the text according to personal beliefs Rank cultural practices according to a continuum Analyze relationships between words
Reading Tasks:	Make predictions Identify main ideas Read for details Research media coverage of courtship and marriage
Writing Tasks:	Write an opinion paragraph Write a letter stating an opinion Describe a cultural tradition of courtship Use related word forms for cohesion Summarize research findings
Vocabulary:	Word definitions Analogies Synonyms and antonyms Word forms
Grammar:	Articles: definite and indefinite

UNIT SUMMARY

This unit explains how choosing a spouse and courtship vary in different cultures. Reading One is an article about courtship and selection of a mate from a journal for students of anthropology. Reading Two is a letter to the editor of a student newspaper in which an international student defends his country's traditional way of choosing spouses.

The companion unit in *NorthStar: Listening and Speaking* deals with one couple's prenuptial agreement and other people's reactions to it.

1 Focus on the Topic, PAGE 175

✪✪✪ A PREDICTING

Suggested Time: 10 minutes

Focus
To get students thinking about marriage and the challenges associated with it by inviting them to discuss a joke about marriage.

Setup
Have the students form small groups (of different ages, if possible) to read the joke and discuss the questions. When the groups have finished, ask a volunteer to explain the meaning of the joke. Then ask students to report their ideas about questions 2 and 3.

Expansion/Homework
(1) You could dictate the joke to students with books closed. Then discuss the joke as a whole class before moving on to questions 2 and 3. (2) Students can respond to question 3 by writing one paragraph as homework. When they return to class, have them share their responses in small groups.

✪✪ B SHARING INFORMATION

Suggested Time: 15 minutes

Focus
To get students to think about what's important to them in choosing a spouse and to share information.

Setup
Have students rate the reasons for choosing a spouse and then discuss their responses in pairs (of different language backgrounds, if possible).

Expansion/Homework
(1) You could assign this exercise as homework, and then have students discuss their ratings. (2) For more writing practice, have students write a paragraph about the reasons for their ratings.

✪✪✪ C **PREPARING TO READ**

BACKGROUND
Suggested Time: 15 minutes

Focus
To stimulate students' interest in differing marriage customs and narrow the topic as students take a quiz matching cultures with marriage practices.

Setup
Have students take the quiz, compare their answers in pairs, and then give them the answers from the Answer Key. Ask them to explain which items surprised them the most.

Expansion/Homework
(1) This quiz could also be assigned as homework. (2) Have students place a "+" next to the statements that are true for their culture and a "–" next to the statements that are false. Then tell them to rewrite the statements that are false so that they are true for their cultures. In groups (of different cultural backgrounds, if possible), have them discuss their statements.

VOCABULARY FOR COMPREHENSION
Suggested Time: 15 minutes

Focus
To introduce marriage-related vocabulary to aid comprehension of Reading One.

Setup
Read the instructions and have the students do the crossword puzzle individually. Then go over the answers using an overhead transparency, if possible. Clarify and give examples as needed.

Expansion/Homework
(1) This exercise could be assigned as homework. (2) After the students complete the puzzle, you could ask them to categorize the words according to parts of speech. This might be helpful because this exercise provides little context.

2 Focus on Reading, PAGE 178

✪✪✪ A **READING ONE: *Finding a Spouse***

Suggested Time: 10 minutes

Focus
To spark students' curiosity about the reading and help them predict the content by relating it to their personal experience.

Setup

If possible, bring in an academic journal and explain how such publications differ from popular magazines. Go over the definition of *anthropology* as you read the introduction. Next, have students discuss the questions with a partner sitting nearby. Then elicit answers from the whole class.

Expansion/Homework

For more writing practice, have students write their answers to the questions within a time limit. Then have them read their answers to a partner sitting nearby. Call on students to describe how they met their spouses or how they hope to meet their future spouses. Use the board to list their ideas.

✪✪✪ READING FOR MAIN IDEAS
Suggested Time: 10 minutes ⏱

Focus

To get students to comprehend the main ideas of the text by matching cultures with cultural beliefs taken from the reading.

Setup

Have students do the matching individually and then check their answers with a partner sitting nearby. As you discuss the answers, point out that many of the cultural beliefs are traditional and may no longer be true.

Expansion/Homework

You could assign this exercise as homework. In addition, you could ask each student to write one traditional cultural belief concerning marriage from their own culture. Ask students to share what they wrote with the class.

Link to *NorthStar: Listening and Speaking*

Ask students to discuss which of these cultures might favor using prenuptial agreements. Have them use information from the reading to support their ideas.

✪✪✪ READING FOR DETAILS
Suggested Time: 25 minutes ⏱

Focus

To get students to examine the text more thoroughly by answering questions about detailed information.

Setup

Have students read the instructions and write their answers individually. When they compare their answers with a partner sitting nearaby, have them discuss any answers that differ until they can agree on the correct answer. Then ask students to share their answers with the class. Offer clarification as needed.

Expansion/Homework

(1) This exercise could be done as homework. Use class time to go over the answers as a whole class. (2) For more writing practice, have students write their answers on the board and do peer correction. Offer comments and feedback as needed.

✪✪ REACTING TO THE READING
Suggested Time: 45 minutes ⏱

Focus
To help students interpret and make inferences from the reading as they match various marriage problems with the culture in which they would most likely occur and the cultural belief related to the problem.

Setup
For Exercise 1, have students read the instructions and work individually. Next, have them compare their answers in pairs (of different language backgrounds, if possible). Then call on individual students to share their answers. Make sure that they support their answers with information from the text. For Exercise 2, review the different ways of finding a spouse that are listed. Then have students respond to the questions in pairs (of mixed cultural backgrounds, if possible). Give the students a time limit for writing the paragraph in class. (Provide the following topic sentence: *In my opinion, the best way to find a spouse is to . . .*) Next, have the students meet in small groups (of mixed language levels) to read their paragraphs to each other. Then call on each group to find out which ways of finding a spouse the students liked best. Keep a tally on the board to determine which ways seem most preferable. Have students explain their reasons for making a particular choice.

Expansion/Homework
(1) Exercise 1 could be assigned as homework. (2) You could have students complete Exercise 1 in pairs or small groups (of different fluency levels) to encourage discussion and reasoning as they complete the assignment. (3) The paragraph-writing task in Exercise 2 can be assigned as homework. Use class time to have students share their paragraphs in small groups.

✪✪✪ B | READING TWO: *What's Wrong with Tradition?*
Suggested Time: 30 minutes ⏱

Focus
To extend the topic of marriage as students read a letter to the editor in which a Vietnamese student defends arranged marriages.

Setup
If possible, bring in a Letters to the Editor section from a magazine or newspaper. Discuss how people write these letters to express their opinions. Next, ask students to read Paul Nguyen's letter individually and then write their responses in the space provided. You may want to write a model response on the board. Then have students share their letters with each other in small groups (of different language backgrounds, if possible). Circulate among the groups to give feedback on language use. Then call on students who agree with Paul Nguyen as well as those who disagree. Ask them to share their responses with the class.

Expansion/Homework
(1) The reading and writing portions of this activity could be done as homework, with the sharing done in the next class. (2) After students have

finished this exercise, you might want to put them in pairs (of different cultural backgrounds, if possible) to do a role play. Have one student play the role of Paul Nguyen and the other play the role of a friend who disagrees with him. In their role play, have them discuss their ideas about choosing a spouse.

✪✪✪ C   LINKING READINGS ONE AND TWO

Suggested Time: 30 minutes

Focus
To get students to synthesize information from both readings as they discuss who makes marriage decisions in various cultures; to compare cultures in terms of how much freedom they allow in choosing marriage partners.

Setup
Have students discuss questions 1 and 2 in small groups (of different fluency levels). Then have them read and complete item 3. Have them discuss their answers in the same small groups, backing up their choices with support from the readings. Then call on the whole class to see if a consensus can be reached concerning the graph. If not, allow room for a variety of interpretations as long as they are supported by the readings.

Expansion/Homework
(**1**) For more writing practice, have students write their answers to questions 1 and 2 before they discuss them in class. (**2**) This writing could be done as homework, along with the graph assignment in item 3. (**3**) You might want to continue the discussion with this question: *Do you think your parents will give you more freedom, less freedom, or the same amount of freedom to choose a spouse as they were given?*

❸ Focus on Vocabulary, PAGE 185

✪ EXERCISE 1
Suggested Time: 15 minutes

Focus
To reinforce and expand the meanings of the words in both readings of this unit by focusing on how these words relate to other words.

Setup
Read the instructions and elicit student examples of each analogy type. Then have students complete the exercise individually before comparing answers with a partner sitting nearby. Encourage discussion of incorrect items to clarify meaning.

Expansion/Homework
You could assign this exercise for homework, and then correct it in class.

Link to *Northstar: Listening and Speaking*

Have students choose five vocabulary items from Unit 10 and use them to create the following types of analogies: synonym, antonym, cause/effect, degree, and related.

✪ EXERCISE 2
Suggested Time: 20 minutes

Focus

To examine vocabulary from this unit in a new context as students categorize statements related to marriage and then arrange them chronologically.

Setup

Read the introductory explanation and then have students do the exercise individually before comparing answers with a partner sitting nearby. Discuss the correct categorization and order with the whole class.

Expansion/Homework

You might want to have groups compete. Prepare by making enough copies of Exercise 2 for as many groups as you will have. Cut each copy into strips so that each item is on one strip. Put each set of strips into an envelope. Divide the class into groups (of varying fluency levels). Put the three categories on the board and explain the activity. Now give each group one envelope and tell them to begin. The first group to finish with the items in correct order wins. Remember to accept variations in the order that may reflect cultural differences.

✪ EXERCISE 3
Suggested Time: 25 minutes

Focus

To give students a chance to use new vocabulary actively in writing.

Setup

Begin by eliciting examples of courtship traditions from the United States and other cultures. Then read the instructions and give students a time limit for writing in class. Circulate among students and offer help as needed. Make note of any grammatical difficulties that arise as students use the new words in writing. Review correct word usage with the whole class as needed.

Expansion/Homework

(1) The writing can be done as homework. Collect the paragraphs and comment on the use of vocabulary. Share outstanding examples with the class. (2) You can post outstanding examples on a class bulletin board or website. (3) Use errors from the writing to create an error correction worksheet. Guide students in using the words clearly and grammatically.

Link to *NorthStar: Listening and Speaking*

Have students choose five or more vocabulary words from Unit 10 and add them to this assignment.

 For extra vocabulary practice, have students work on the self-grading vocabulary activities for the unit on the NorthStar Companion Website at **http://www.longman.com/northstar**.

4 Focus on Writing, PAGE 187

✪✪✪ A   STYLE: Using Related Word Forms for Cohesion

Suggested Time: 20 minutes 🕐

Focus

To guide the students as they practice the effective use of related word forms in sentences about marriage.

Setup

Read the introduction and then have students look at the two paragraphs in Exercise 1 with a partner to determine what makes them cohesive. After reading the next explanation, have students fill in the blanks in the sentences as instructed in Exercise 2. Elicit answers and list them on the board. Next, ask students to work with a partner sitting nearby to write three sentences using related word forms. Then call on various pairs to write their sentences on the board for comments and correction.

Expansion/Homework

You might want to assign Exercise 2 for homework and then correct it in class.

Link to *NorthStar: Listening and Speaking*

Have students write about prenuptial agreements using related word forms from Unit 10.

✪✪ B   GRAMMAR: Articles—Definite and Indefinite

Suggested Time: 20 minutes 🕐

Focus

To help students use definite and indefinite articles in a paragraph about planning a wedding.

Setup

Have students work with a classmate sitting nearby to examine the paragraph in Exercise 1 and identify the indefinite and definite articles as directed. Encourage students to share what they know about these forms. Next, have them read the grammar explanations silently before working independently to complete Exercise 2. Then have them compare their answers with a classmate sitting nearby. Go over the answers as a whole class and discuss any questions students have.

Expansion/Homework

(1) This entire section works well as homework. (2) For more writing practice, you could ask students to interview a partner about a marriage-related custom. Then have each student write a paragraph about the custom, using definite and indefinite articles as modeled in Exercise 2. Create an error correction sheet from examples of students' misuse of articles. (3) For further practice, offer

exercises from *Focus on Grammar, Intermediate* and from *Fundamentals of English Grammar*. See the Grammar Book References on Student Book page 193 for specific units and chapters.

 For extra practice in the writing process, have students go to the *NorthStar Writing Activity Book, Intermediate*.

✪✪✪ C | WRITING TOPICS

Focus
To integrate the vocabulary, concepts, grammar (definite and indefinite articles), and style focus (using related word forms for cohesion) of the unit in a short writing assignment.

Setup
Assign this exercise for homework, perhaps allowing several days.

Expansion/Homework
You might want to have students exchange papers with a partner and look for a good topic sentence (underline it), one effective use of related word forms (circle it), and one effective detail (put a star in front of it).

Link to *NorthStar: Listening and Speaking*
Encourage students to use the vocabulary from Unit 10 in their writing.

✪ D | RESEARCH TOPICS

Focus
To give students a chance to explore the topic of marriage in newspapers and magazines.

Setup
Bring in newspapers and magazines to show the class. If possible, bring in a bridal magazine. Read the instructions and make sure students understand what to look for. If possible, show an example of each item on the list. Next, go over the questions to be used in writing the summary and give the students time to write it outside of class. Then place them in small groups (of students who work well together) to share their summaries. Circulate among groups, taking note of interesting findings that can be shared with the whole class.

Expansion/Homework
(1) You could also have students use the Internet to find marriage-related websites. Have them use the list of items in Step 1 as a guide.

Link to *NorthStar: Listening and Speaking*
Have students search magazines, newspapers, and websites for information related to prenuptial agreements.

Student Book Answer Key

UNIT 1

BACKGROUND, page 2
1. F
2. T
3. F
4. F

VOCABULARY FOR COMPREHENSION, page 3
2. market
3. goal
4. campaign
5. message
6. global
7. convince
8. competition
9. succeed
10. fail

READING FOR MAIN IDEAS

1 page 5
Sentence 3: When advertisers write an ad, their goal is to make people want to buy the product.

Sentence 4: Laws about advertising are different all over the world.

2 page 6
Answers will vary. Suggested answers:

1. Jacko is an Australian football player who appeared in the battery ads. His failure in the United States campaign shows that advertisers need to change their campaigns when they advertise in different countries.
2. The translation could be wrong. A wrong translation may send the wrong message.
3. The global advertiser must pay attention to different communication styles as well as different laws and customs.
4. A company should do this because people in different countries have different likes and dislikes.

READING FOR DETAILS, pages 6–7
1. a
2. c
3. b
4. b
5. c
6. d
7. d
8. b

REACTING TO THE READING

1 page 8
2. 4, c
3. 4, a
4. 1, b
5. 3, c

C LINKING READINGS ONE AND TWO, page 11
Answers will vary.

3 FOCUS ON VOCABULARY

1 page 12
2. b
3. c
4. b
5. d
6. d
7. c
8. a

2 page 13
1. c
2. e
3. f
4. g
5. d
6. a
7. h
8. b

A STYLE

1 page 14
1. The main ideas are found in the first and last sentences.
2. The examples are found in the second and third sentences.
3. There are four examples.

2 page 15
1. D3
2. D1
3. D2
4. TS
5. CS

B GRAMMAR

1 page 15
You're waiting and *are changing* are present progressive, and *think* and *enjoy* are simple present.

2 page 16
1. believe
2. is increasing
3. serve
4. consider
5. are writing / write
6. make

UNIT 2

BACKGROUND, page 20
1. c
2. d
3. a
4. b

VOCABULARY FOR COMPREHENSION, page 21
1. b
2. b
3. a
4. a
5. b
6. b
7. a
8. b
9. a
10. b

READING FOR MAIN IDEAS, page 24
1. F
2. T
3. F
4. F
5. F
6. T

READING FOR DETAILS, page 24
Suggested answers:

1. He landed the 900, a difficult trick.
2. He spent 13 years practicing it.
3. He began skateboarding when he was about 10 years old.

4. He learned to ride a skateboard at the Oasis Skate Park.

5. He had problems with jocks who picked on him, and he also had problems sitting still in class.

6. His son saw his tricks in a Tarzan movie.

REACTING TO THE READING

☐1 page 25

Answers will vary. Suggested answer:

Mom: He's only happy when he gets something right.

Dad: Do you remember how he practiced every day after school?

Mom: Looking back now, I guess that helped him because he had so much energy.

Dad: That's our Tony—a real professional.

☐2 page 25

Answers will vary.

B READING TWO

☐2 page 27

1. a   3. a   5. a
2. b   4. b

C LINKING READINGS ONE AND TWO

☐2 page 28

Answers will vary.

A – family pressure

T, A – desire to be the best

T – childhood experiences

A – peer pressure

3 FOCUS ON VOCABULARY

☐1 page 28

NOUN	VERB	ADJECTIVE	ADVERB
1. *accomplishment*	accomplish	*accomplished*	X
2. escape	*escape*	*escaped*	X
3. *controversy*	X	controversial	*controversially*
4. benefit	*benefit*	*beneficial*	*beneficially*
5. *obsession*	*obsess*	*obsessive*	obsessively
6. *intensity*	*intensify*	intense	*intensely*
7. perfection	*perfect*	*perfect*	*perfectly*
8. *practice*	*practice*	practiced	X

☐2 page 29

1. obsessed   5. obsessive
2. obsession   6. escape
3. intense   7. hooked on
4. awesome   8. benefit

4 FOCUS ON WRITING

☐4 pages 30–31

who—Fact #1

when—Fact #2

where—Fact #3

why—Fact #4

what—Fact #5

B GRAMMAR

☐2 page 32

1. can   6. could
2. be able to   7. be able to
3. can't   8. be able to
4. couldn't   9. Can
5. could

UNIT 3

VOCABULARY FOR COMPREHENSION, page 37

1. a   4. c   7. c   10. c
2. b   5. c   8. b   11. a
3. b   6. a   9. a

READING FOR MAIN IDEAS, pages 40–41

2. c, 2   4. b, 8   6. c, 4
3. b, 5   5. a, 6

READING FOR DETAILS, page 41

2. f, 5   4. c, 4   6. e, 2
3. d, 2   5. b, 6   7. a, 6

REACTING TO THE READING

☐1 page 41

1. F   3. T
2. T   4. F

B READING TWO

☐2 page 42

Answers will vary. Suggested answers:

1. Reading Two is an advertisement for a cancer clinic named the Organic Health Center.

2. He claims that he learned the causes and cure of cancer as he traveled around the world. In fact, however, he has no real medical training.

3. It is a special diet consisting of herbs combined with healthy foods.

C LINKING READINGS ONE AND TWO

1 page 43

2. Their products are good for many illnesses.

3. They offer money-back guarantees.

4. They invite you to read testimonials

5. They promise quick, exciting cures.

6. The product/treatment is made in a secret way and is only available from them.

7. They say that doctors and/or the rest of the medical community are against them.

2. __1__ "My health center offers the most advanced treatments for curing cancer and other diseases."
   __5__ Program C: For all diseases"

3. __7__ "I provide a money-back guarantee if the program fails."

4. __6__ " . . . I have testimonial letters for you to read."

5. __4__ "After one to six months on this diet, you will be cured of cancer."

6. __2__ "This cure is available only at the Organic Health Center."

7. __3__ "That's why doctors will tell you not to trust me."

2 page 44

Answers will vary. The important task for the students is to be able to give good reasons based on the readings for their answers. Those who practice Western medicine would probably choose 3 and 7 as the "real treatments."

3 FOCUS ON VOCABULARY

1 page 44

Circle all words except likable *and* knowledgeable.

2 pages 45–46

1. offered
2. unproven
3. guarantee
4. discovery
5. fraud
6. founder
7. mistake
8. victim of
9. harmless
10. lie

3 page 46

Answers will vary.

A STYLE

2 page 47

1. SD2
2. SD5
3. SD4
4. SD3
5. SD6
6. SD1

Many people are using quacks instead of doctors. Unfortunately, these people often don't realize how dangerous it is to use a quack. It is dangerous because the product usually doesn't work. As a result, the patient's illness can be getting worse during the treatment. People often go to quacks because they want an easy solution for their problems and because they are afraid. Quacks understand this. So they sell products for illnesses that have no cure, and people who are afraid of dying will pay any price for them. It can be difficult to know if someone is a quack, but there are ways. Quacks use similar techniques for selling their products. If you are concerned about buying something from a quack, there are people and organizations that can help you.

3 page 48

Answers will vary.

B GRAMMAR

1 1. The statements in 1b. and 2b. are stronger than those in 1a. and 2a. because they use superlative adjectives.

2 page 50

1. the worst
2. the most educated
3. the most intelligent
4. the easiest
5. the best
6. the fastest
7. the most dedicated
8. the most helpful
9. the healthiest

UNIT 4

VOCABULARY FOR COMPREHENSION

1 page 55

Answers will vary. Possible answers:

2. passed out
3. quickly took
4. banging
5. unpleasant
6. material
7. calmed
8. fearless
9. stinky
10. worthless
11. succeeded in finishing
12. know

2 page 56

1. g
2. j
3. a
4. l
5. h
6. e
7. c
8. b
9. i
10. k
11. d
12. f

READING FOR MAIN IDEAS, page 60

Answers will vary. Suggested answers:

1. Gregor has become an insect.
2. His family is frightened when they see Gregor.
3. Only his sister takes care of him, but she eventually stops.
4. He dies in his room as he thinks of his family.
5. His family feels relieved when he dies.

READING FOR DETAILS, page 60

2. Gregor panicked and said, "No, no, I will come out immediately."

3. The manager began to back out of the room to leave, and Gregor realized he couldn't let him go.

4. He slid under the couch and slept there until morning.

5. The next morning, Gregor's sister looked in and was surprised to see that he hadn't eaten a thing.

6. The first few didn't hurt him, but then one pierced his body, and he felt terrible pain.

7. His sister also began to care less and less about feeding him and cleaning his room.

8. We must find a way to get rid of this thing.

REACTING TO THE READING

1 page 61
Answers will vary. Suggested answers:

1. T: "Gregor, are you all right? Do you need anything?"

2. F

3. T: Gregor panicked and said, "No, no, I will come out immediately. I was sick, but now I feel much better."

4. T: At the sight of him, the manager screamed, his mother fainted, and his father wept.

5. T: The family now left his door to the dining room open for two hours every night after dinner, and he could listen to their conversation. He really loved this.

6. T: His sister also began to care less and less about feeding him and cleaning his room.

B READING TWO

2 page 64
Answers will vary. Suggested answers:

1. The critics think this story is funny because of how Gregor learns to move his insect legs and body. It is sad because his family stops loving him when he becomes disgusting.

2. He wanted to use something that would represent Gregor as weak, cowardly, rough, and disgusting.

3. Gregor is weak and disgusting because he hates his job and doesn't want to work to pay off the family debt. His family is like a parasite to him. By becoming a cockroach, Gregor becomes the parasite to his family, helpless and having no responsibility.

4. Gregor becomes the disgusting son that nobody cares about. His family rejects him, while he loves them to the end.

3 FOCUS ON VOCABULARY

2 pages 64–65
Answers will vary. The important task for the students is to become aware that while some synonyms have very similar

meanings, others have elements both of similarity and dissimilarity.

3 page 66

Across	Down
2. brave	1. screamed
4. managed to	3. couch
6. soothed	5. cockroach
9. metamorphosis	7. useless
10. Grab	8. beat

4 page 67
Answers will vary.

A STYLE

1 page 68
Answers will vary. Possible answers:

2. supervisor started
3. put (it) in his mouth / awful
4. to enter
5. to ask / murder

2 page 69
Answers will vary. Possible answers:

1. I'm getting out of bed now.
2. because his father didn't work any longer.
3. They did not comprehend anything he said.
4. This must stop.
5. Again his mother yelled, while the manager quickly left.

B GRAMMAR

2 page 70

2. f	4. a	6. b
3. g	5. c	7. e

3 pages 70–71

2. His family locked Gregor in his room to keep him there.

3. His father grabbed a walking stick and newspaper to beat Gregor.

4. Grete went into Gregor's room every day to feed him.

5. Gregor followed Grete into the dining room to help her.

6. Gregor came out of his room to listen to the music.

7. His family took a train ride to celebrate his death.

UNIT 5

VOCABULARY FOR COMPREHENSION, page 75

2. a	4. c	6. a	8. a	10. c
3. b	5. c	7. b	9. a	11. b

READING FOR MAIN IDEAS, page 79

2. T
3. T
4. F: Gender differences . . . when they **play.**
5. F: Differences in language . . . are **different** in all cultures.
6. F: **Boys** gain status . . .
7. T
8. F: **Women** usually talk more . . . than **men** do.

READING FOR DETAILS, page 79

		Paragraph
2.	a	1
3.	b	2
4.	b	4
5.	a	5
6.	c	7
7.	a	9
8.	c	10

REACTING TO THE READING

1 pages 80–81

		Paragraph
1.	a	1
2.	c	2
3.	b	6
4.	c	4,5
5.	b	3
6.	a	6
7.	a	8
8.	a, b	9, 10, 11

C LINKING READINGS ONE AND TWO, page 83

1. F	3. M	5. F	7. F	9. M
2. M	4. F	6. M	8. F	10. F

3 FOCUS ON VOCABULARY

1 page 83

MALE: waiter, butler, host, garbage man, salesman, steward, repairman

FEMALE: stewardess, maid, seamstress, waitress, hostess

UNISEX: garment worker, sanitation worker, server, salesperson, flight attendant, repair person

2 page 84

1. gender
2. compete
3. masculine
4. feminine
5. fair
6. influence
7. reflects
8. emphasizes, proves
9. status
10. prove, emphasize

A STYLE

2 pages 86–87

1. Joy loves jumping rope with her two best friends. Tommy, in contrast to Joy, likes to play ball with a large group of boys.
2. Tommy enjoys telling the other boys what to do. Joy, on the other hand, doesn't like it when new girls join her friends.
3. Boys might play in large groups in which every boy knows his place. Girls, however, usually play in smaller groups.
4. Boys compete with one another for leadership. Unlike boys, most girls want other girls to like them, and this is more important to them than winning.
5. A woman may be annoyed when her husband simply tells her how to solve the problem. Likewise, a husband may be annoyed when his wife wants to stop and ask a stranger for directions.

B GRAMMAR

1 1. b   2. a   3. b

2 page 88

2. Can you come over to my house?
3. Could you tell me about Lisa?
4. Could you come over here and listen to my problem?
5. Would you mind stopping the car so I can ask for directions?

3 page 89

Answers will vary. Suggested answers:

1. Could you send me one of your catalogues?
2. Could I please have a copy of my baby's sonogram?
3. Could you please send me a copy of my bill?
4. Could I please have two tickets for your next play?

UNIT 6

VOCABULARY FOR COMPREHENSION, page 95

1. F	4. T	7. F	10. F
2. T	5. T	8. F	11. F
3. F	6. F	9. T	12. T

READING FOR MAIN IDEAS

2 page 98

_2_ Antarctica has no government.

_3_ The entire world may be affected by problems in Antarctica.

_1_ Many different scientists learn new things by studying Antarctica.

READING FOR DETAILS

1 page 98

I. Scientists learn new things in Antarctica because it is different from other places.
   a. oldest ice in the world
   b. Unique view of space
   c. Very harsh environment

II. Problems in Anartica may affect the world.
   a. Large ozone hole above Antarctica.
   b. Ice = 70 percent of the earth's fresh water.
   c. Vast fields of ice = Earth's air conditioner

2 pages 98–99

Suggested answers:

2. The writer wants Antarctica to be closed to tourists.

3. Psychologists study how people behave when they live and work in Antarctica.

4. The oil spill caused by a cruise ship killed many penguins.

5. Tour companies may not be concerned about the environment of Antarctica.

6. If we don't stop tourism in Antarctica, there may be consequences for everyone on Earth.

7. The ice of Antarctica reflects sunlight and cools the Earth.

REACTING TO THE READING

1 page 99

1. a	4. b
2. a	5. a
3. a	6. b

C LINKING READINGS ONE AND TWO

1 page 102

Suggested answers:

Opinions of the Scientist

3. Tourists ask questions and take scientists away from their work.

Opinions of the Tourist

2. Tourists can be given rules to follow that will protect the environment.

4. Tourists appreciate Antarctica very much, and they understand that it is a unique place.

3 FOCUS ON VOCABULARY

1 page 103

Answers will vary. Suggested answers:

unique: landscape, continent, weather, sea birds, tourism

coastal: oil spill, landscape, weather, ice, temperature

harsh: landscape, weather, global warming, effect, consequences

vast: oil spill, landscape, continent, global warming, ozone hole

remote: oil spill, continent, ice, sea birds

fragile: continent, ice, sea birds

frozen: landscape, continent, ice

oldest: tourists, continent, ice, sea birds, landscape, research

scientific: consequences, research

natural: landscape, consequences, effect, temperature, ice

2 pages 103–104

2. C/E-a
3. S-b
4. A-a
5. N-b
6. U-b
7. D-b
8. A-c
9. D-a
10. S-a

3 pages 104–105

Answers will vary. Suggested answers:

2. Why should we preserve Antarctica?

3. What are the negative effects of tourism on Antarctica?

4. How do the vast ice fields of Antarctica help us?

5. Why is the ozone layer important?

6. What could be a consequence of global warming?

7. How can we protect the fragile environment of Antarctica?

8. What are some people concerned about?

4 FOCUS ON WRITING

2 page 106

Answers will vary. Suggested answers:

The Introduction

1. "And although I can appreciate their desire to experience this beautiful landscape, I feel Antarctica should be closed to tourists."

2. The author is a scientist studying the age of ice in Antarctica, and his work is interrupted by tourists.

The Body

3. Paragraph 2: Antartica is the center of important scientific research, and it must be preserved for this purpose.

   Paragraph 3: When tourist groups come here, they take us away from our research.

   Paragraph 4: The need to protect Antartica from tourists becomes even greater when we consider the fact that there is no government here.

   Paragraph 5: If we don't protect Antartica from tourism, there may be serious consequences for us all.

4. reasons why tourism is harmful, examples of mistakes tourists make, and facts about the environment

5. explanation of Antarctica's lack of governmental protection

The Conclusion

6. "The only way to protect this fragile and important part of the planet is to stop tourists from traveling to Antarctica."

7. It makes a prediction about the future by describing the possible consequences of destroying the environment of Antarctica, and it suggests that tourists be stopped from traveling to Antarctica.

3 page 107
Answers will vary.

B GRAMMAR

2 page 109

2. The biologists were taking showers while we were eating lunch.
3. I cried when I got off the boat.
4. Many sailors lost their lives while they were trying to sail around South America.
5. We were running and jumping on the iceberg when it started to break.
6. The tourists arrived while the scientist was working on an experiment.

UNIT 7

BACKGROUND, page 115
Predictions will vary.

VOCABULARY FOR COMPREHENSION, page 116

1. b	4. a	7. h	10. k
2. c	5. d	8. j	11. g
3. e	6. i	9. f	

READING FOR MAIN IDEAS, page 120

		Paragraph
1.	T	1
2.	F	3
3.	F	4
4.	T	7
5.	T	8
6.	T	6

READING FOR DETAILS, page 120

1. c	3. b	5. a
2. c	4. b	6. b

REACTING TO THE READING

2 page 121
Answers will vary. Suggested answers:

1. Lucille Ball
2. Lucille Ball, Lucy Ricardo
3. Lucy Ricardo
4. Lucille Ball, Lucy Ricardo
5. Lucy Ricardo
6. Lucille Ball
7. Lucy Ricardo

B READING TWO

2 pages 123–124
Answers will vary. Suggested answers:

1. The parents are both professionals, and they seem to love each other. There are five children of different ages, and the grandparents are part of the family.

2. It shows a perfect, happy family that deals with ordinary human problems with a good sense of humor.

C LINKING READINGS ONE AND TWO

1 page 124
Answers will vary. Suggested answers:

1. Ricky was always strong and kept his dignity, but Cliff sometimes showed weakness. Lucy stayed home and took care of her family, but Clair worked outside the home.

2. *Answers will vary.*

2 page 125
Answers will vary. Suggested answers:

When I played Lucy Ricardo, women <u>were usually housewives</u>.

Now we have the Cosby wife as an example of a woman who <u>has her own professional career</u>.

On the other hand, *The Cosby Show* gives people a chance to see a family that <u>was dealing with common problems</u>.

I think it is important now when we can be so divided by differences of <u>race and money</u>.

I know he enjoyed slapstick, so he might think *The Cosby Show* <u>isn't very funny</u>.

One thing I know he would like is how *The Cosby Show* <u>has a main character, Cliff, who likes to chuckle</u>.

3 FOCUS ON VOCABULARY

1 page 126

Suffixes

–ity	–ion	–ing	–ed
dignity	ambition	encouraging	comforted
opportunity	tension	charming	henpecked
	imperfection	frustrating	confused
		satisfying	well dressed
		comforting	limited

–ous	–able
humorous	unforgettable
tremendous	believable

–ity	–ion	–ing	–ed	–ous	–able
noun	noun	adjective	adjective or verb	adjective	adjective

2 pages 126–127

Answers will vary. Suggested answers:

2. She found encouragement in a dream.
3. You must be ambitious if you want to be a successful doctor like Cliff Huxtable.
4. There was tension in the *I Love Lucy* audience when Lucy got in trouble.
5. Ricky Ricardo was always dignified even when his wife played tricks on him.
6. *I Love Lucy* and *The Cosby Show* were both TV shows that had humor.
7. One of the things that made *I Love Lucy* and *The Cosby Show* successful was that people identified with Cliff and Lucy as imperfect people.
8. Ricky was satisfied with his career as a bandleader.
9. Although Lucy knew that Ricky loved her, she also knew that his patience had a limit.
10. We identify with Cliff's imperfections, and it is comforting for us to see that someone loves him anyway.

4 FOCUS ON WRITING

2 page 129

Answers will vary. Suggested answers:

1. *I Love Lucy* was exciting and surprising to watch.
2. The show's writers worked carefully and closely together.
3. Theo's sisters and parents think that he is irresponsible with money.
4. We identify with Cliff's imperfections and are comforted to see that someone loves him anyway.
5. In a perfect world, both husband and wife have satisfying, high-paid careers, time and energy to love their kids, and the ability to laugh.

6. If we chuckle our way through our problems and love the people around us, things are going to be OK.
7. I just noticed that a certain person said, "Can I borrow that jacket?" and then proceeded to wear that jacket every single day.
8. All episodes are based on real day-to-day problems and handle the problems with humor.

3 page 130
Answers will vary.

B GRAMMAR

2 pages 131–132
Answers will vary. Suggested answers:

1. Betty wants to know who Lucy is.
2. Betty wants to know what her neighbor's name is.
3. Lucy knows when Ricky usually comes home, and this makes her nervous.
4. Betty asks where Ricky works.
5. The *I Love Lucy* show is what Mary and Betty are watching together.
6. Wanting to be in show business is why Lucy tries to work in the nightclub.

3 page 132
Answers will vary. Possible answers:

6. Simple family happiness is why the critics said *The Cosby Show* would be a hit.
7. What the TV critic said was interesting to me because I agree that we are divided by money and race.
8. I want to know how Cliff and Clair had time for two careers and five children.

UNIT 8

BACKGROUND, page 136
Answers will vary.

VOCABULARY FOR COMPREHENSION, page 137

1. permanent
2. popular
3. modern
4. traditional
5. slim
6. height
7. weight
8. admire
9. desire
10. attractive
11. appearance
12. ideal

READING FOR MAIN IDEAS, page 140

a. 2
b. 8
c. 3, 6
d. 7
e. 5
f. 8

READING FOR DETAILS, page 140

1. T
2. F: During the time of the French Revolution, women wanted to have smaller waists.
3. T
4. T
5. T
6. F: Liposuction is often used to remove body fat.
7. F: Cosmetic surgery has been used for centuries in China and India.
8. T
9. F: Some women tried to reshape their mouths by repeating words that started with the letter "p."
10. T
11. F: Cosmetic surgery is expensive for the average person.

REACTING TO THE READING

☐1 page 141

Answers will vary. Suggested answers:

1800s: American women admired French fashions because they made women look attractive.

1890s: People who rode bicycles wanted to look and feel better.

1990s: Men who lose their hair can have it replaced.

2025: Cosmetic surgery will be safer, faster, and less expensive.

C LINKING READINGS ONE AND TWO, page 145

Suggested answers:

1. He can have his hair replaced.
2. She can have a face-lift, or she can use makeup.
3. She can have liposuction, or she can diet and exercise.
4. He can have rhinoplasty, or he can use permanent makeup.
5. She can have cosmetic surgery to improve her appearance.

3 FOCUS ON VOCABULARY

☐1 page 146

Answers will vary.

2. modern/traditional: music, appearance, surgery, color, style, relationship, man, makeup
3. popular: music, surgery, hair, color, personality, style, man, makeup
4. attractive: appearance, hair, color, personality, style, weight, height, body, man, makeup
5. slim: appearance, style, body, man
6. permanent: surgery, color, relationship, makeup
7. fashionable: music, appearance, surgery, hair, color, style, weight, relationship, height, body, man, makeup
8. painful: surgery, relationship, body

☐2 pages 146–147

Answers will vary.

A STYLE

☐2 pages 148–149

1. As a result
2. since
3. Thus
4. because
5. Consequently
6. therefore
7. as
8. as a result

☐3 page 149

Answers will vary.

B GRAMMAR

☐2 page 151

1. used to
2. used to
3. used to
4. didn't use to

UNIT 9

VOCABULARY FOR COMPREHENSION, page 157

1. f
2. i
3. k
4. a
5. l
6. b
7. j
8. d
9. g
10. c
11. h
12. e

READING FOR MAIN IDEAS, page 159

1. B
2. A
3. B
4. B
5. B
6. A
7. B
8. B
9. A
10. B

READING FOR DETAILS, page 160

b. 10
c. 6
d. 8
e. 9
f. 1
g. 2
h. 4

REACTING TO THE READING

☐1 page 160

Answers will vary.

☐2 page 161

Suggested answers:

Author of "Life in Prison is Still Life Why Should a Killer Live?"

- believes in fairness
- cares about victims
- wants to protect society

☐3 page 161

Suggested answers:

Author of "Why Do We Kill People to Show That Killing People Is Wrong?"

- believes freedom is important
- believes mistakes are unusual
- hopes that people will change

4 page 161

Suggested answers:

Pro

1. An executed murderer will never murder again.

2. An executed murderer will not be able to enjoy life.

3. An executed murderer will not have to be supported in prison with tax money.

4. Execution sends a strong message to others that murderers will be punished.

Con

1. It teaches people that forgiveness is unnecessary.

2. An innocent person might be executed by mistake.

3. Poor people and minorities are executed more often than whites.

4. Execution costs more tax money than keeping a person in prison for life.

5. People can change for the better while they are in prison, and execution takes away this hope.

B READING TWO, page 162

Graph 1

1. 2002

2. 20 countries (Answers to the second question may vary.)

3. Against. More countries have abolished the death penalty or have not used it for decades.

4. *Answers will vary.*

Graphs 2 and 3

5. It dropped because people were given another choice: life imprisonment without parole.

6. More people support life imprisonment than capital punishment.

Graph 4

7. (Suggested answer) It shows that innocent people have been imprisoned or executed by mistake.

8. *Answers will vary.*

C LINKING READINGS ONE AND TWO, pages 164–165

Answers will vary. Suggested answers:

1. In 2002, 55 percent of voters in Albany County, NY, said in a survey that they agree with capital punishment.

2. In the 1900s, 23 innocent people were executed by the United States government, and 327 innocent people were going to be executed but were released from prison.

3. (Pro) Eighty-four nations allow capital punishment today. (Con) One hundred eleven nations have abolished capital punishment or have not used it for decades.

3 FOCUS ON VOCABULARY

1 page 165

Mark the following A.

3. misunderstanding
4. anger
5. punishment
6. justice
9. citizenship
10. innocence
12. government
13. guilt
14. society
15. rights

2 page 166

1. h		6. b
2. f		7. e
3. a		8. d
4. i		9. c
5. j		10. g

3 pages 166–167

1. executes (stronger)
2. criminal (weaker)
3. cruel (stronger)
4. loved ones (stronger)
5. citizens (stronger)
6. foreigners (neither)
7. destroy (stronger)
8. revenge (stronger)

4 FOCUS ON WRITING

2 page 169

1. Wayne Paulson was the kind of guy that was never noticed at school and never got into trouble.

2. Since the police came to his house and arrested Wayne for murder, his life has never been the same.

3. Because Wayne was found guilty at the end of his trial, he was given the death penalty.

4. Wayne said that he is innocent, but the jury didn't believe him.

5. Although his life in jail is very different now, Wayne still remembers his life before jail.

6. Wayne's mother doesn't want him to feel lonely, so she visits him almost every day.

7. Some prisoners like Wayne are able to leave prison if they get new trials.

8. Wayne asks about getting a new trial when his lawyer visits him.

3 pages 170–171

Answers will vary. Suggested answers:

1. We've been discussing capital punishment, and my classmates and I have really been shocked by some of the statistics we've learned.

2. The United States has executed ten since 1990, and it plans to continue to execute child criminals.

3. I used to agree with capital punishment because I always thought that the fear of the death penalty stopped some criminals, but that is false.

4. . . . between 1900 and 1992, 350 criminals were sentenced to death. They were later found to be innocent.

5. Although some of the prisoners are innocent, they get executed because there is no perfect way to find out if someone is guilty.

B GRAMMAR
2 pages 172–173

1. has been
2. has been waiting
3. has been writing
4. has been
5. have visited
6. has been coming
7. has always believed
8. has been telling
9. has loved

UNIT 10

BACKGROUND, page 176
Answers will vary. Suggested answers:

1. g
2. c
3. b
4. g
5. e
6. a
7. d

VOCABULARY FOR COMPREHENSION, page 176

Across
2. pregnancy
5. background
6. raise
7. community
8. leadership
9. fertility
10. produce

Down
1. romantic
3. characteristics
4. spouse

READING FOR MAIN IDEAS, page 180

1. d
2. b
3. e
4. a
5. c

READING FOR DETAILS, pages 180–181
Suggested answers:

1. A matchmaker helped by finding someone of the right age and background.

2. A successful marriage was one that produced sons.

3. They stopped night visits if they thought a boy might not be a good husband.

4. They believe that unmarried women should not get pregnant.

5. He believed that group marriage was the best form of marriage.

6. In the past, the Mormons allowed one man to have several wives, but now they believe that marriage should be limited to one man and one woman.

REACTING TO THE READING
1 page 181
Suggested answers:

1. Chinese—It's more important to have sons.

2. Bavarian—A woman must show her fertility before she can get married.

3. Oneida Community—Group marriage is the best way for men and women to live together.

4. Mormon (in the past)—A man should have several wives.

5. Chinese—Young people should not be allowed to choose their own marriage partners.

6. Hopi—A boy can only see a girl if her parents think that he will be a good husband.

B READING TWO, page 184
Answers will vary.

C LINKING READINGS ONE AND TWO, pages 184–185
1 and 2. *Answers will vary.*
3. *Answers will vary. Suggested answers:*

a. 8
b. 8
c. 1
d. 1
e. 4
f. 1

3 FOCUS ON VOCABULARY
1 pages 185–186

2. R-c
3. A-a
4. C/E-a
5. D-c
6. R-a
7. D-a
8. C/E-c

2 pages 186–187

a. W-5
b. C-2
c. M-10
d. W-7
e. M-8
f. C-1
g. W-6
h. M-9
i. C-4
j. C-3

4 FOCUS ON WRITING
2 pages 188–189

1. similar
2. married
3. marriage
4. court
5. courtship
6. traditional
7. romance
8. tradition
9. romantic
10. similarity

B GRAMMAR
2 page 190

1. a
2. the
3. a
4. a
5. a
6. a
7. a/the
8. a
9. the
10. The

Unit Word List

The **Unit Word List** is a summary of key vocabulary from the Student Book's Vocabulary for Comprehension and Focus on Vocabulary sections. The words are presented by unit, in alphabetical order.

Unit 1

all in a row
all over the place
campaign (noun)
come in overnight
competition
convince
fail
firm (noun)
global
go over well
goal
have a hard time
look at the big picture
market (noun)
market (verb)
message
succeed
take one's time
translation
will/would not hear of
yell

Unit 2

accomplish
accomplishment
awesome
beneficial
benefit (noun)
controversial
controversy
decent
escape (noun)
freak (noun)
get by
get hooked on
get it right
intense
intensely
jocks
land (verb)
make it
obsessed
obsession
obsessive
perfect (verb)
practice (verb)

Unit 3

Prefixes		
il- / im- / ir-	mis-	un-
Suffixes		
-able / -ible	-less	

arthritis
clinic
discovery
founder
fraud
guarantee
harmless
helpless
hopeless
improper
irregular
irresponsible
knowledgeable
lie (verb)
likable
make a mistake
miracle
misunderstand
misused
offer (noun)
quack
qualified
unable
undecided
unpopular
unproven
victim

Unit 4

awful
beat (verb)
brave
certainly
comprehend
couch
cry
disgusting
enter
faint (verb)
grab
knock
manage to
panic
pierce
realize
scream
smelly
soothe
stinky
substance
support (verb)
surely
tap
terrible
thick
understand
useless
weep

Unit 5

butler
compete
emphasize
fairly
feminine
flight attendant
garbage man
garment worker
gender
gossip (verb)
host
hostess
identity
influence (verb)

maid
masculine
prove
reflect
repair person
salesperson
sanitation worker
seamstress
server
status
steward
stewardess
waiter

Unit 6

ancient
astronomer
be concerned about
coastal
consequences
continent
crisis
decrease
delicate
effect
expertise
fact
flood
fragile
frozen
global warming
harsh
huge
ice
increase
inhabitant

inhabited
landscape
natural
oil spill
oldest
ozone hole
preserve
rare
remote
research
result
scientific
sea birds
telescope
temperature
tourism
tourist
unique
vast
vast ice field
weather

Unit 7

Suffixes					
-able	-ed	-ing	-ion	-ity	-ous

ambition
ambitious
believable
bicker
charming
comforted
comforting
confused
deal with
dignified
dignity
encouragement
encouraging
flirt with
frustrating
henpecked

humor
humorous
imperfect
imperfection
limit
limited
mean (adjective)
opportunity
satisfied
satisfying
scene
stunt
tension
tremendous
unforgettable
well dressed

Unit 8

admire
appearance
attractive
beautiful
body
desire (noun)
fashionable
hair
height
ideal
make-up (noun)
mentally
modern

painful
permanent
personality
physical
physically
popular
relationship
slim
style
surgery
traditional
weight

Unit 9

act
anger
chance
citizen
citizenship
crime
criminal (noun and adjective)
cruel
dangerous
destroy
execute
fair
fairness
foreigner
forgiveness
government
guilt
guilty
hurt (verb)
immigrant
immigration
innocence
innocent
justice
killer
lifestyle
loved ones
message
misunderstanding
murder
murderer
prison
punishment
respect
revenge
right (noun)
society
violent

Unit 10

attracted to
background
characteristics
community
courtship
divorce
enduring
engagement
everlasting
feature
fertility
infertility
leadership
many
marriage
matchmaker
partner
partnership
pregnancy
produce (verb)
raise
romantic
similar
spouse
unique
wedding ceremony

Introduction to Achievement Tests

The following reproducible Achievement Tests allow teachers to evaluate students' progress and to identify any areas where they might have problems developing their reading and writing skills. The Achievement Tests should be given upon completion of the corresponding Student Book unit.

Description   There are two Achievement Tests for each unit. **Test 1** is a "paper and pencil" test of receptive skills. It assesses students' mastery of reading comprehension and of the vocabulary, style, and grammar points introduced in the unit.

Test 2 is intended to assess the students' productive, or writing, skills. It consists of a writing task related to the content of the unit. Each writing task is designed to elicit a writing sample of one or more paragraphs.

Administration   Both tests should be taken in class. When taking the tests, students should not be allowed access to any *NorthStar* materials or to their dictionaries. Students should be able to complete either **Test 1** or **Test 2** within 30 minutes or less of class time.

Teachers can decide how to incorporate **Test 2** (the writing task) into their testing situations. Some teachers will assign each writing task immediately after students complete **Test 1**; others may decide to set aside another time to complete it. Because students will be completing other writing assignments as part of their work in *NorthStar,* teachers may not find it necessary to assign each of the **Test 2** writing tests. Instead they may choose to measure their students' writing progress by administering only some of the tests; for example, they may decide to give every other test or a total of three or four over the term.

Scoring Test 1   Individual test items are worth one point, for a maximum total of 30 points per test. To facilitate scoring, an answer key is provided at the end of this test section. A student's score can be obtained by adding together the number of correct items. To obtain an overall "reading score" for a student, teachers may average all of the **Test 1** scores that the student received.

Scoring Test 2   The writing tasks are evaluated holistically using the categories in the rating sheet that follows. The categories include content, vocabulary, organization, and grammar. In each category, 0 indicates poor or inadequate performance for the level; 1 indicates average or acceptable performance; 2 indicates good or outstanding performance. The teacher circles the rating for each category and adds the numbers to obtain a total score out of a possible 8 points.

```
┌─────────────────────────────────────────┐
│ Test 2 Rating Sheet                       │
│                                           │
│ Student: _____  Unit _____    │
│                                           │
│ Content            0      1      2        │
│                                           │
│ Vocabulary         0      1      2        │
│                                           │
│ Organization       0      1      2        │
│                                           │
│ Grammar            0      1      2        │
│                                           │
│ ┌───────────┐                             │
│ │ Total Score│ _____           │
│ └───────────┘                             │
└─────────────────────────────────────────┘
```

The teacher can complete the rating sheet for each student's test and give it to the student. It can also be kept by the teacher as a record of each student's progress.

An overall "writing score" for a student may be obtained by averaging all of the **Test 2** scores the student received in the class.

TestGen CD-ROM Packaged in the back cover of this *Teacher's Manual and Achievement Tests* is a test generator CD-Rom that allows teachers to create and customize their own *NorthStar* tests from the 300 **Test 1** questions on the reproducible tests, and from the **Test 2** writing tasks.

Achievement Tests
Unit 1

TEST 1

A. *Read the excerpt.*

For many years any kind of commercial advertising in China was illegal. Government advertising was all over the place, but business advertising was nonexistent. Then Sony came along and changed things. The Japanese companies were the first to start advertising in China. They've led the way for others to come into the country. We can learn something from them, too. It's important not to come in overnight and start advertising right away. Advertisers must take their time and plan their campaigns carefully. Because there are millions of people in China who don't know what a Big Mac is, you wouldn't want to rush over there and try to sell them one. Instead, you would want to plan ahead five or ten years. It pays to be patient in China.

Now, in Russia, you would have to think about your product and whether or not there's a market for it. Fast food, for example, is a very strange idea in Russia. In their restaurants, you sit down and the waiter brings you soup, salad, meat, and potatoes: one item at a time. The Russians think of food as something you take your time with, something you enjoy.

1 *Write **T** (true) or **F** (false) for each main idea.*

_____ **1.** For a long time, businesses couldn't advertise in China.

_____ **2.** When the Japanese first started advertising in China, they didn't take their time.

_____ **3.** Russians aren't very interested in food.

2 *Circle the answer that best completes each sentence.*

1. Government advertising in China _____.
   a. couldn't compete
   b. wasn't allowed
   c. was everywhere

2. Japanese companies were successful in China because they _____.
   a. started advertising immediately
   b. planned their campaigns carefully
   c. changed the government's policy

3. Before McDonald's can sell a lot of hamburgers in China, the company needs to _____.
   a. make changes to their product first
   b. inform customers about their product
   c. sell their product for five to ten years

4. At first, Russians thought fast food was strange because they _____.
   a. were used to being served
   b. didn't like the taste
   c. preferred to eat at home

B. *Complete each sentence with the correct word from the list.*

competitive	fail	goal	message	translation
convince	firm	global	succeed	yell

1. When you try to advertise a product in a new country, be careful about the language. Your ad may not work because of _____ problems.

2. Intertek is a company that has offices in over 30 countries. It's truly a _____ organization.

3. John works for a small _____. It only has 20 employees.

4. I saw an ad for a new kind of breakfast cereal. The _____ of the ad was this: if you eat the cereal every day, you will have more energy and lose weight.

5. Most companies want to sell more of their products. That's their _____.

6. When I play sports, I like to win. In other words, it's important to me to _____.

7. You don't have to _____. I can hear you perfectly.

8. There are over 20 companies trying to sell bottled water, so the market is very _____.

9. My friend tried to get me to buy a different car, but he couldn't

_____ me.

10. Janet is terrified of taking the test because she's afraid she will

_____ .

C. *Write the idiom from the list that best completes each sentence.*

hear of it	all in a row	take your time
go over too well	have a hard time	all over the place

1. We didn't see any commercials for 40 minutes, and then we saw five of

them _____ .

2. Jacko's angry campaign didn't _____ in the United

States.

3. I wanted to take a sales trip to Japan, but my boss wouldn't

_____ .

4. I've seen that model's face before. Her ad's _____ .

5. You can't rush a new advertising campaign. You need to

_____ .

6. If you don't understand a country's culture, you'll

_____ selling products there.

D. *Identify each sentence below. Label the topic sentence (**TS**), the examples (**D1, D2**), and the concluding sentence (**CS**).*

_____ 1. For example, when Braniff Airlines' advertisement for its fine leather
seats was translated from English to Spanish, it told people they
could fly naked!

_____ 2. To avoid these kinds of problems, most advertisers are beginning to
write completely new ads for each market.

_____ 3. Also, Chevrolet tried to market the Chevy Nova in Latin America,
but nobody bought the car because *no va* in Spanish means
"doesn't go."

_____ 4. As companies become more global, they must consider differences in
language and culture when they advertise around the world.

E. *Complete the paragraph with the correct form of the verbs. Use the simple present or the present progressive. Use contractions when possible.*

My boss _____ that our company's ad campaign _____
        1. (think)   2. (not, help)

our current sales. Therefore, the management _____ ideas for a
                                               3. (discuss)

new ad. My boss _____ that a new ad will definitely increase
                            4. (believe)

sales. He _____ a pay raise to the employees with the best ideas.
                  5. (offer)

TEST 2

Write a paragraph about an unsuccessful advertisement you've seen.

- Where did you see the advertisement? (on TV, in a magazine or newspaper, etc.?)

- What is the ad trying to sell?

- Why doesn't it work?

Achievement Tests
Unit 2

TEST 1

A. *Read the excerpt.*

Dr. Paula Kim, director of the Eating Disorders Clinic at Baldwin Hospital, explains that it is not unusual for athletes, especially gymnasts, to become obsessed with their weight. One reason is this: in gymnastics, the lighter the body, the more skillfully it can perform. She explains that an obsession with weight can lead to extreme dieting, which affects not only the body but also the mind.

"For the anorexic, the mental focus becomes very small: food and weight. In a way, it's easy to see how this helps the anorexic manage the fear of living in the big, uncontrollable world out there. You may not be able to control how other people feel about you, but you can control what you put in your mouth. You can also control how many hours you spend at the gym. Soon you get hooked on controlling your weight."

1. *Write T (true) or F (false) for each main idea.*

_____ **1.** Athletes exercise a lot, so they don't usually worry about their weight.

_____ **2.** Extreme dieting has effects on the mind as well as the body.

_____ **3.** Anorexics lose weight because they don't think much about food.

_____ **4.** For an anorexic, eating becomes a way of controlling others.

2. *Circle the answer that best completes each sentence.*

1. Gymnasts are often _____ concerned than other athletes about their weight.

   a. more   **b.** less

2. For some athletes, losing weight has become an _____.

   a. extreme   **b.** obsession

3. The anorexic has many _____.

   a. interests   **b.** fears

4. Anorexics feel that they don't have enough _____ in their lives.

   a. control   **b.** exercise

B. *Circle the best definition for the underlined word in each sentence.*

1. George felt like a <u>freak</u> in high school. He didn't have many friends.
   a. strange person   **b.** popular person

2. After learning how to ski, I <u>got hooked on</u> it. Now I ski every year.
   a. got tired of   **b.** got very interested in

3. I like to practice something until I <u>get it right</u>.
   a. can focus on it   **b.** can do it really well

4. Exercise has many <u>benefits</u>. It's good for your body and mind.
   a. goals   **b.** rewards

5. Steve thinks his uncle is <u>awesome</u>. He loves to spend time with him.
   a. amazing   **b.** weird

6. Did you <u>land</u> the 900?
   a. fail at   **b.** succeed at

7. Many of my friends in high school were <u>jocks</u>.
   a. athletes   **b.** good students

8. I feel really tired. I'm not sure I'm going to <u>make it</u>.
   a. start   **b.** finish

9. Were you able to <u>get by</u> in school?
   a. do OK   **b.** do really well

10. Some people use exercise as <u>an escape from</u> their problems.
    a. a way out of   **b.** a way to understand

C. *Complete each sentence with the correct form of the word.*

1. Bill won first prize in the skating contest. It was quite an

   _____ .
       (accomplish)

2. Stop worrying about your weight. You're being _____
                                                      (obsession)
   about it.

3. It took Tony Hawk 13 years to _____ the 900.
                                        (perfectly)

4. Donna was lucky in school. She was a _____ student.
                                              (gift)

5. Some people don't like skateboarding. It's a _____ sport.
                                                    (controversy)

6. Becoming a great athlete takes _____ concentration.
$\qquad$ (intensity)

7. Eating lots of fruits and vegetables is _____ for your health.
$\qquad$ (benefit)

D. *Write the word or phrase that best completes each sentence.*

1. That's an amazing trick! I _____ believe it!
$\qquad$ (can / can't)

2. When I was younger, I _____ skateboard all day.
$\qquad$ (able to / could)

3. My mother _____ understand why I loved it so much.
$\qquad$ (couldn't / wasn't able to)

4. I haven't _____ land the 900 yet.
$\qquad$ (could / been able to)

5. My dream is to _____ ride a skateboard like Tony Hawk.
$\qquad$ (be able to / can)

TEST 2

Write a paragraph about someone you admire.

- Who is this person?

- Why do you admire him or her?

Achievement Tests
Unit 3

Name: _____

Date: _____

TEST 1

A. *Read the excerpt.*

When people are faced with medical problems, the first place they usually go to is their doctor's office. But, increasingly, the next stop for medical information is the Internet. The Internet offers a wide variety of websites that provide information and support for people with almost any medical problem.

However, the Internet has also become a way for quacks to advertise their miracle cures. Some websites that say they are offering medical information are actually trying to sell you something. Don't become the victim of medical fraud; that is, don't believe everything you read on the Internet. Here is some advice to help you avoid becoming a victim of medical fraud on the Internet:

- When you are searching for information, go to the websites of well-known universities or clinics. Remember that anyone can make up a professional-sounding name for their website, but the website may have no connection to a real organization.

- Look carefully at the source of information. If the site offers proof of a new discovery, find out who made the discovery and who tested the drug.

- Beware of testimonials. Testimonials are the personal stories of satisfied customers. Testimonials are very easy to invent, but it is usually impossible to find out if they are real.

1 *Circle the answer that best completes each main idea.*

1. The Internet has become a popular _____ of medical information.

   a. object   **b.** website   **c.** source

2. However, people shouldn't _____ all of the medical information found on the Internet.

   a. trust   **b.** like   **c.** prove

2 *Write **T** (true) or **F** (false) for each detail.*

_____ 1. Quacks sometimes advertise on the Internet.

_____ 2. Some websites are actually trying to sell you something.

_____ 3. Testimonials are difficult to make up.

_____ 4. All websites with professional-sounding names are reliable.

_____ 5. There are websites for almost any medical problem.

_____ 6. You can usually trust information from a well-known university or clinic.

B. *Read the paragraphs below. Then complete each sentence with the correct word from the list.*

arthritis   guarantee   quack
clinic   harmless   qualified
discovery   miracle   unproven
fraud   offer   victim

It is terrible to be a _____ of _____. I
                              1.   2.
know. Here's my story . . .

I was looking for a _____. I had had a pain in my neck
                           3.
for months. My joints were sore. I thought I had _____. I
                                                           4.
read about a doctor who had made an important _____ and
                                                        5.
had opened a _____ for treatment. I knew the treatment was
                     6.
_____ because the doctor could only _____
        7.   8.
testimonials from people who had had the treatment; there were no results
from any real scientific studies. But I went anyway. It cost $3,500 for a
week! Since there was no _____, I knew I couldn't get my
                                  9.
money back if the treatment didn't work. The doctor and his staff seemed
_____. They were very professional. The end of the story is
        10.
that the treatment didn't work. I lost my money. The doctor was a
_____. Luckily, the treatment was _____. It
        11.   12.
didn't hurt either. Yesterday, I went out and bought myself a new pillow. It
cost $25. Guess what? I woke up this morning without any pain in my neck!

C. *Complete each sentence with the correct form of the word. Use one of the prefixes or suffixes from the list.*

PREFIXES	SUFFIXES
un-	-less
ir-/il-/im-	-able/-ible
mis-	

1. Few quacks are _____ about medical treatments.
   (knowledge)

2. It's _____ to sell many drugs without a doctor's prescription.
   (legal)

3. This is a new treatment. It's still _____.
   (tested)

4. People who are _____ about a cure are more likely to buy
   (hope)
   quack medicines.

5. Quack doctors can _____ their power over desperate
   (use)
   patients.

D. *Complete the sentences. Use the superlative form of the adjectives. Don't forget to use* **the**.

1. Dr. Davis is one of _____ sports medicine doctors in the
   (good)
   world.

2. He is also one of _____ men I have ever met.
   (intelligent)

3. He is not a quack. He uses _____ treatments known to
   (advanced)
   medicine.

4. Dr. Davis treats some of _____ sports injuries.
   (bad)

5. His clients are among _____ athletes in the world.
   (famous)

TEST 2

Write two or three paragraphs about the best way to get medical information.

- How do you get medical information (for example, from your doctor, the Internet, magazines, newspapers, etc.)?

- What do you think are the best ways to get medical information?

- Why do you prefer these sources?

Achievement Tests
Unit 4

Name: _____

Date: _____

TEST 1

A. *Read the excerpt.*

Gregor grew tired of being in the bedroom day and night, and soon took to walking back and forth across the walls and ceiling. It felt much better than walking on the floor. His sister noticed this because of the brown sticky substance left from his feet wherever he walked. She decided to move most of the furniture out of the room to make more walking space for Gregor. But Gregor wanted to keep a picture on the wall: a picture of a beautiful woman dressed in pretty clothes. While Grete and her mother were in the other room, he quickly climbed the wall and pressed himself against the picture to stop them from taking it. When his mother saw him, she screamed and fainted. His sister then became very angry with him. He followed her into the dining room to help her, but this frightened her. When his father returned home and learned what had happened, he became very angry. Gregor tried to return to his bedroom to get away from his father, but he was unsuccessful. He couldn't fit through the doorway.

1 *Circle the answer that best completes each main idea.*

1. Gregor tried to _____ .
   a. help his sister
   b. move a picture
   c. run out of the house

2. Gregor's family was _____ .
   a. worried about him
   b. upset with him
   c. fond of him

2 *Write **T** (true) or **F** (false) for each detail.*

_____ 1. Gregor walked on the ceiling.

_____ 2. His sister took out most of the furniture.

_____ 3. His family put the picture in the dining room.

_____ 4. Gregor talked with his mother and sister.

_____ 5. He was able to get away from his father.

B. *Match the underlined word in each sentence with its synonym below. Write the correct letter.*

_NO_ 1. Don't <u>panic</u>! It's just the doorbell.

_____ 2. Bill's parents will <u>support</u> him as long as he stays in college.

_____ 3. The clock doesn't work any more. It's <u>useless</u>.

_NO_ 4. The room was never cleaned, so the dust became <u>thick</u> on the floor.

_NO_ 5. This situation is impossible. We can't <u>go on</u> like this.

_____ 6. We don't have much time. <u>Grab</u> your books and let's go!

_____ 7. If you stand up too quickly, you may <u>faint</u>.

_____ 8. The wall was covered with a white, chalky <u>substance</u>.

_____ 9. I had a sore throat, so I took some medicine to <u>soothe</u> the pain.

_NO_ 10. When she saw the murder, the woman began to <u>scream</u>.

_NO_ 11. Please <u>whisper</u>. The baby's asleep.

_____ 12. Your bedroom is a mess. It's <u>disgusting</u>.

p55 beating ✓
✓disgusting
✓brave
✓smelly managed to realize

a. give money to	**d.** no good	**g.** take	**j.** be afraid
b. speak softly	**e.** continue	**h.** relieve	**k.** yell
c. lose consciousness	**f.** material	**i.** heavy	**l.** terrible

C. *Circle the best paraphrase for each sentence.*

1. Gregor finally managed to open the door.
   a. Gregor tried to open the door.
   b. Gregor kept opening the door.
   c. Gregor was able to open the door.

2. Something pierced his body.
   a. Something went into his body.
   b. Something attached itself to his body.
   c. Something slid off his body.

3. He took to climbing the walls.
   a. He wanted to climb the walls.
   b. He often climbed the walls.
   c. He was tired of climbing the walls.

4. Gregor rocked back and forth.
   a. Gregor shook from end to end.
   b. Gregor moved from top to bottom.
   c. Gregor rolled from side to side.

5. He thought of his family tenderly.

   a. He had kind feelings toward his family.
   b. He got worried about his family.
   c. He was very hurt by his family.

6. Gregor was found dead by his family.

   a. Gregor's family found him before he died.
   b. Gregor's family found him while he was dying.
   c. Gregor's family found him after he died.

D. *Complete the answers to the questions using the cues in the list. Use an infinitive of purpose in each answer.*

>   steal some money
>   go on a trip
>   lose some weight
>   wake up the children
>   keep it from crying

1. Q: Why was the woman beating on the door?

   A: She was beating on the door _____.

2. Q: Why did the robber go into the bank?

   A: He went into the bank in order _____.

3. Q: Why did John buy the plane tickets?

   A: He bought the tickets _____.

4. Q: Why was she holding the baby?

   A: She was holding the baby in order _____.

5. Q: Why did the man go on a diet?

   A: He went on a diet _____.

TEST 2

Imagine that you have been changed into a cockroach or some other insect. Write two or three paragraphs about your life as an insect.

- What kind of insect are you?

- How does it feel to be this insect?

- How do people react to you?

Achievement Tests
Unit 5

Name: _____

Date: _____

TEST 1

A. *Read the excerpt.*

> **GIGI JONES (GJ):** I know you've written a lot about gender and language, Dr. Speakwell.
>
> **DR. SPEAKWELL (DS):** Yes, I have. I find it very interesting. For example, you just called me "Doctor." That used to always suggest a man, not a woman.
>
> **GJ:** Maybe I should call you "Doctorette."
>
> **DS:** Actually, I prefer to be called "Doctor."
>
> **GJ:** Why is that?
>
> **DS:** Well, you know, English has several feminine words that people sometimes use when they're referring to women. You probably know them, right? Poetess, songstress, bachelorette? Now these words aren't used too often, but they exist in the language. However, some women don't like such words because they feel as if these words make them seem less important than men.
>
> **GJ:** What do you mean by that?
>
> **DS:** For instance, if you say the word "actress," people don't always think of a serious artist. They might think of some silly, beautiful female who's more worried about her makeup than she is about Shakespeare. But when you say "actor,"—that's not silly at all. That's a serious word, a respectable word.

☐1 *Write **T** (true) or **F** (false) for each main idea.*

_____ 1. The endings *–ette* and *–ess* are frequently used in English.

_____ 2. Women sometimes don't like words with feminine endings because they seem less serious than words without them.

_____ 3. To most people, acting is not a respectable profession.

☐2 *Complete the chart.*

Male	Female
_____ 1.	doctorette
poet	_____ 2.
bachelor	_____ 3.
_____ 4.	actress

B. *Circle the answer that best completes each sentence.*

1. Every society defines _____ somewhat differently.
   a. masculine   **b.** gender   **c.** sex at birth

2. According to Deborah Tannen, the way men and women talk _____ these differences.
   a. studies   **b.** receives   **c.** reflects

3. For example, American boys like to _____ about how well they can do things.
   a. boast   **b.** compete   **c.** play

4. Most American girls try to _____ their friends by using less direct language.
   a. influence   **b.** command   **c.** emphasize

5. A girl who has popular friends may have high _____.
   a. leadership   **b.** circle   **c.** status

6. Differences between adult men and women sometimes cause _____ problems.
   a. discussion   **b.** communication   **c.** knowledge

7. When a woman talks to a man about a problem, she wants to know that he feels _____ for her.
   a. solution   **b.** sympathy   **c.** annoyed

8. For women, talking with their friends is an important part of _____.
   a. friendship   **b.** gossip   **c.** identity

9. When women speak, they use more _____ forms than men.
   a. language   **b.** direction   **c.** polite

10. Men and women who learn more about each other may be able to improve their _____.
    a. rules   **b.** relationships   **c.** differences

C. *Choose the transition that best completes each sentence.*

1. Boys like to compete. They _____ like to lead.
   (also / however)

2. For men, friendship means doing things together.
   _____, for women, it means being able to talk
   (On the other hand / Similarly)
   frequently with their friends.

3. _____ men, who say things directly, women prefer
   (In contrast to / Also)

   to use indirect language.

4. _____ a man, who would simply say, "Come
   (Unlike / Likewise)

   here," a woman might say, "Could you please come here?"

5. Women are taught language that is socially appropriate for their gender.

   _____, men are taught language that is socially
   (On the contrary / Likewise)

   appropriate for their gender.

6. A girl might receive a pink dress or a doll as a gift.

   _____, a boy might receive a book or a football.
   (However / Unlike)

7. English has masculine and feminine word forms.

   _____, Japanese has masculine and feminine word
   (Similarly / In contrast to)

   endings.

D. *Unscramble the words in a.–f. to make sentences. Then write the letter of the unscrambled
sentence that best completes each situation. Punctuate your sentences correctly.*

   a. (I/could/a/you/question/ask/?)

   _____

   b. (me/pass/the/could/you/butter/?)

   _____

   c. (go/my/to/house/let's/.)

   _____

   d. (me/throw/ball/the/.)

   _____

   e. (mind/would/the/you/tickets/getting/?)

   _____

   f. (isn't/this/store/a/great/it/is/?)

   _____

Situations

1. Betty is going to a play with Louise Saturday night. She e-mails Louise about getting the tickets. She asks, _____

2. You're a student and you don't understand something in class. After class you ask the teacher, _____

3. Barbara is with a group of her friends. She wants them to come to her house. She says, _____

4. John and Paul are playing football. John wants the ball. He says, _____

5. Carol is eating dinner with her parents. She wants some more butter. She asks, _____

6. Sue is shopping in a store with her friends. She likes the store. She says, _____

TEST 2

Write your opinion about the following statement: "Culture plays a bigger role in determining gender than biology."

- What does this statement mean?

- Do you agree or disagree with it? Explain.

Achievement Tests
Unit 6

Name: _____

Date: _____

TEST 1

A. *Read the excerpt from the travel journal.*

Detaille Island, Antarctica   **February 28**

    While we were crossing the Antarctic Circle, we were drinking champagne to celebrate the day. Each year, only 300 visitors come this far south. Mark explained that the ice is blue down here because it catches all the colors of the rainbow except for blue. I have always thought of Antarctica as nothing but white. But now I see a clear blue light shining through the mountains of ice all around us, and I have no words to describe the beauty.

    Our ship passed a huge field of frozen sea. Mark invited us to come out and play. We weren't sure at first, but when we felt how solid it was, we jumped and ran. All around us were mountains and glaciers that no one has ever explored. It amazed me to think that no human hand or foot has ever touched them; only a few human eyes have seen them.

    When I get home, it will be hard for me to explain what the feeling of amazement was like, but I will try.

    We all felt sad today when we realized that our ship was heading north. We really don't want to leave Antarctica—a unique world.

1. *Circle the answer that best completes each main idea.*

    1. Their ship is _____ Antarctica.
        a. going toward   **b.** going away from

    2. The ice in Antarctica is _____ .
        a. blue and white   **b.** nothing but white

    3. When their ship passed a frozen sea, they _____ .
        a. got off the ship   **b.** stayed on the ship

2. *Write **T** (true) or **F** (false) for each detail.*

    _____ **1.** The ice in Antarctica reflects all the colors of the rainbow.

    _____ **2.** The writer thinks Antarctica is very beautiful.

    _____ **3.** The people in the ship were the first people to see these mountains and glaciers.

    _____ **4.** The writer is sorry to be leaving.

B. *Complete each sentence with the correct word from the list.*

coastal	fragile	landscape	remote
consequence	harsh	ozone hole	tourists
continent	inhabited	preserve	vast

1. Tom's vacation cabin was so _____ that it was difficult to find.

2. One _____ of global warming may be changing patterns of rainfall.

3. During our train ride across the country, we enjoyed looking at the _____.

4. A lot of American _____ visit Europe every summer.

5. Siberia is so _____ that it crosses several time zones.

6. We need to _____ the rain forests for the many birds that live there.

7. Because of the _____ over Australia and New Zealand, the people there need to be careful about exposing themselves to the sun.

8. The plants are so _____ that they can easily be destroyed by people walking on them.

9. Asia is the world's largest _____.

10. _____ cities are more popular vacation spots than inland cities.

11. Few plants can live in Antarctica as a result of the _____ climate.

12. Some of the older cities in the Middle East have been _____ for thousands of years.

C. *Circle the word that best completes each analogy.*

1. old : new = near : _____

ancient   close   remote

2. warm : water = frozen : _____

air   ice   cold

3. live : inhabit = difficult : _____

stay   harsh   easy

4. writer : essay = scientist : _____

effect   report   opinion

5. vast : huge = trash : _____

problem   garbage   tourist

6. cold weather : snow = rain : _____

ice   floods   sunlight

7. hurt : kill = damage : _____

destroy   increase   protect

D. *Complete each sentence with the correct form of the verb. Use the simple past or the past progressive.*

1. Last year, my wife and I _____ a trip to New York.
                                            (take)

2. During the flight, I was watching the movie while my wife _____
                                                                      (listen)
to music.

3. When we _____ at the airport, we saw our friends.
                    (arrive)

4. We found out about their news while we _____ for our baggage.
                                                   (wait)

TEST 2

Write several paragraphs about the most "remote" place you ever visited.

- Where was it?
- Why did you go there?
- What did you like (or dislike) about the experience?

Achievement Tests
Unit 7

Name: _____

Date: _____

TEST 1

A. *Read the excerpt.*

Cliff and Claire Huxtable. They are the loving African-American parents of five children: four girls and one boy. They live in a nice big house filled with pretty furniture. They are well-dressed, and their children, ranging in age from preschool to high school, are bright and charming. Grandma and Grandpa are part of the fun, too. What's so funny about that? It's quite simple. Cliff and Claire show us family life in America not as it is, but as it could be. In a perfect world, both husband and wife have satisfying, high-paid careers. They still have time and energy to love their kids, and when pressures build up, they are able to laugh. Dr. Huxtable is here to show us that yes, life is a little frustrating at times, but if we chuckle our way through our problems and if we love the people around us, things are going to be OK.

1 *Write **T** (true) or **F** (false) for each main idea.*

_____ **1.** The Huxtables are an unhappy family.

_____ **2.** Most American families are like the Huxtables.

_____ **3.** Dr. Huxtable has a sense of humor.

2 *Circle the word or phrase that best completes each detail.*

1. The Huxtable family consists of _____.

   a. parents and   **b.** parents, children,
   children   and grandparents

2. Mrs. Huxtable _____.

   a. stays home with   **b.** has a job outside
   the children   the home

3. The Huxtable children _____.

   a. are of different ages   **b.** have trouble in
                                  school

4. When the Huxtables have problems, they _____.

   a. laugh about them   **b.** don't pay attention

B. *Complete each sentence with the correct word from the list.*

ambition	dignity	limited	opportunity
bicker	flirt	mean	stunts

1. Jerry's _____ is to get a good job and make lots of money.

2. If you behave with _____ even in difficult situations, people will always respect you.

3. Mary likes to _____ and have fun with the boys in her class.

4. I hate it when couples _____ with each other. Often, they don't even know what they're arguing about.

5. Carla is sometimes _____ to her younger sisters. She teases them and makes fun of them.

6. You need to be very strong and brave to perform _____ in movies.

7. When my grandmother was young, there was less _____ for women in business than there is today.

8. I never believed that my life was _____ in any way. I always thought I could do anything.

C. *Complete each sentence with the correct form of the word.*

1. In *The Cosby Show*, Cliff and Claire Huxtable are a _____
   (love)
   couple.

2. Cliff isn't _____, but he manages to see the humor in things.
   (perfection)

3. *The Cosby Show* was popular because the characters were so

   _____.
   (believe)

4. In *I Love Lucy*, Fred is a _____ husband.
   (henpeck)

5. Part of the humor of the show comes from the _____
   (tense)
   between Fred and his wife, Ethel.

6. The characters of Ricky and Lucy Ricardo are _____.
   (charm)

D. *Complete each sentence with a word or phrase from the list. Make sure each sentence has parallel structure.*

prepare them to be good citizens	saving money
an excellent wife	hard-working
takes care of the family	

1. Amanda is beautiful and _____.

2. She is a good mother and _____.

3. She works during the day and _____
   in the evening.

4. Amanda and her husband want to give their children a good education
   and _____.

5. By working hard and _____,
   they will be able to accomplish their goals.

E. *Complete the answers with noun clauses. Use the information in the questions.*

1. Q: What did Alex do last night?
   A: I don't know _____.

2. Q: How do you feel?
   A: It isn't important _____.

3. Q: Where are they going?
   A: Hmm. Maybe Donna knows _____.

4. Q: What does Sara want?
   A: _____ is to go to college.

TEST 2

Write several paragraphs about your favorite comedian or comedy show.

- What is the name of the comedian (comedy show)?

- Why do you like the comedian (comedy show)?

- Can you give an example of humor used by that comedian (on the comedy show)?

Achievement Tests
Unit 8

Name: _____

Date: _____

TEST 1

A. *Read the excerpt.*

In the past, tattoos (permanent ink drawings on the skin) were associated with a rough life of hard work and danger throughout the Western world. For example, tattoos made people think of the groups of people who tended to wear them, such as sailors, prisoners, and members of motorcycle gangs. In addition, tattoo shops were found only in the bad parts of town, and most people did not find them attractive.

Recently, the image of tattoos has changed dramatically. Today, it is common for young men and women from all parts of society to get tattoos. Tattoos have become a fashion accessory, like a nice pair of earrings or a stylish haircut. At the same time, tattoos today are much more varied than the pictures of women or American eagles that used to be so popular. A modern young person might get a tattoo of a natural image, such as an animal or a flower, or a piece of tattoo "jewelry," where a design is tattooed around a person's arm or neck like a bracelet or necklace.

Is the current popularity of tattooing just a fad? It is difficult to say. Perhaps in the future, it will again pass out of fashion with young people, and only the older generation will have tattoos.

1 *Write **T** (true) or **F** (false) for each main idea.*

_____ 1. Tattooing used to be more popular than it is now.

_____ 2. Today, tattoos have a different association from the one they had in the past.

_____ 3. Today, tattoo images are varied, and young people wear them as if they were fashion accessories.

2 *Circle the word or phrase that best completes each detail.*

1. Tattoos used to be associated with people who had _____ lives.
   a. successful   **b.** difficult

2. In the past, most people thought that tattoos were _____.
   a. ugly   **b.** beautiful

3. A tattoo bracelet is something that can be found _____.
   a. in a jewelry store   **b.** around someone's arm

4. In the future, tattooing may become _____ again.
   a. unfashionable   **b.** permanent

B. *Match the underlined word(s) in each sentence with an adjective from the list.*

a. attractive	**c.** modern	**e.** permanent	**g.** popular
b. fashionable	**d.** painful	**f.** physical	**h.** slim

_____ 1. Diet and exercise can help you improve your <u>body's</u> appearance.

_____ 2. Today's fashion magazines are more <u>liked</u> than ever before. They are read by millions of women around the world.

_____ 3. Charles likes <u>up-to-date</u> furniture with clean, simple lines.

_____ 4. After the surgery, I had an <u>uncomfortable</u> feeling in my chest for several weeks.

_____ 5. Getting a tattoo can have a <u>lasting</u> effect on your appearance.

_____ 6. Bart is tall, muscular, and very <u>good-looking</u>.

_____ 7. Janice really knows how to dress. She always looks <u>stylish</u>.

_____ 8. Fashion models are usually tall and <u>thin</u>. Clothes just seem to look better on this type of body.

C. *Circle the noun that best completes each sentence.*

1. Everyone wants to have short hair these days. That's the popular _____.
   a. appearance   **b.** style

2. Plastic _____ has made it possible for people to improve the way they look.
   a. surgery   **b.** makeup

3. For me, the ideal _____ is about 150 pounds. When it's more than that, I look too heavy.
   a. height   **b.** weight

4. Kim is bright, funny, and charming. She has the best _____ of anyone I know.
   a. personality   **b.** relationship

5. I like to wear traditional _____; it's much more comfortable than a modern business suit.
   a. shape   **b.** clothing

6. It's difficult to make a dramatic change in your life unless you have a strong _____ to do so.
   a. application   **b.** desire

D. *Write the transition that best completes each sentence.*

　　1. Karen has a closet full of beautiful, stylish clothes. _____,
　　　　　　　　　　　　　　　　　　　　　　　　　　(Since / As a result)
　　　she never has a problem finding something nice to wear.

　　2. Some people don't have plastic surgery _____ it's still pretty
　　　　　　　　　　　　　　　　　　　　　(consequently / because)
　　　expensive.

　　3. Black and tan are my favorite colors; _____, I have several
　　　　　　　　　　　　　　　　　　　　　(therefore / as)
　　　black and tan outfits.

　　4. _____ Margaret is overweight, she shops for clothes that
　　　　　(Since / Thus)
　　　make her look thinner.

　　5. People will always want to look beautiful. _____, there will
　　　　　　　　　　　　　　　　　　　　　　　(Consequently / Because)
　　　always be fashion.

E. *Complete each sentence with **used to** or **didn't use to**.*

　　1. In the 1700s, women wanted to look very thin. Therefore, they
　　　_____ wear corsets to make their waists look smaller.

　　2. Until recently, women always wore dresses. They _____
　　　wear pants.

　　3. In North America, women _____ eat arsenic. They did this
　　　to make their faces white.

　　4. Cosmetic surgery _____ be common. It has become much
　　　more popular these days.

TEST 2

Write several paragraphs about the things that make a person attractive.

● What makes a person attractive?

● Which is more important—clothes or personality?

● How can a person make himself or herself more attractive?

Achievement Tests
Unit 9

TEST 1

A. *Read the excerpt.*

In the 1920s there were two sons of rich men; their names were Leopold and Loeb. The two killed a young boy, and then told police that they were the murderers. They were guilty, and everyone knew it. But were they executed? No—their fathers paid for the services of Clarence Darrow, the country's best lawyer. With Mr. Darrow's help, Leopold and Loeb received a punishment of life in prison.

Some citizens were angry about that because of the cruelty of the murder. For the family of the murdered boy, the sentence showed how wealthy people are often able to avoid punishment. No one knows if the relatives of the murdered boy were ever able to offer their forgiveness to Leopold and Loeb. But it is a well-known fact that the two men were sorry for what they had done. Leopold spent the rest of his life caring for sick people. Loeb showed good citizenship by following all the rules in prison and helping other prisoners learn how to read.

1 *Circle the word or phrase that best completes each main idea.*

    1. Leopold and Loeb were _____.
- **a.** innocent
- **b.** punished
- **c.** executed

    2. To the parents of the murdered boy, the sentence was _____.
- **a.** appropriate
- **b.** angry
- **c.** unfair

    3. Leopold and Loeb tried to _____ what they had done.
- **a.** forget about
- **b.** make up for
- **c.** justify

2 *Write T (true) or F (false) for each detail.*

Leopold and Loeb _____.

_____ 1. were brothers

_____ 2. admitted their guilt

_____ 3. went to prison

_____ 4. forgave the murdered boy's relatives

B. *Read the arguments for and against capital punishment. Complete each sentence with a word from the list.*

act	execution	killer	murder
chance	fair	lifestyle	type
cruel	innocent	message	victims

FOR

1. Murderers shouldn't have more rights than their _____.

2. Prisoners are able to enjoy life, and this is not _____.

3. The _____ in many prisons is too comfortable.

4. Taxpayers should not have to pay to keep a _____ alive.

5. Execution sends a strong _____ to others who might kill.

6. People who commit _____ give up the right to live.

AGAINST

1. People who kill aren't always _____.

2. Capital punishment is a _____ of murder itself.

3. _____ people may be executed by mistake.

4. Killing a murderer is a violent _____.

5. The threat of _____ doesn't stop people from committing murder.

6. Life in prison gives people a _____ to change.

C. *Read the pairs of sentences. Circle the best way to combine each pair.*

1. Jason Rivers is hiding from the police. He just murdered his wife.
   a. Jason Rivers is hiding from the police **and** he just murdered his wife.
   b. Jason Rivers is hiding from the police **because** he just murdered his wife.

2. The police have been looking for Rivers. They found out about the murder.

   a. The police found out about the murder, **and** they have been looking for Rivers.

   b. **Although** the police found out about the murder, they have been looking for Rivers.

3. The police found Rivers. They took him to the police station.

   a. **When** the police found Rivers, they took him to the police station.

   b. The police found Rivers, **but** they took him to the police station.

4. Rivers was very nervous. The police became suspicious.

   a. Rivers was very nervous, **so** the police became suspicious.

   b. Rivers was very nervous, **when** the police became suspicious.

5. The police asked Rivers questions. Rivers wouldn't answer them.

   a. The police asked Rivers questions, **since** he wouldn't answer them.

   b. The police asked Rivers questions, **but** he wouldn't answer them.

6. Jason Rivers may be found guilty. Jason Rivers may go to prison.

   a. **If** Jason Rivers is found guilty, he will go to prison.

   b. Jason Rivers may be found guilty **because** he may go to prison.

D. *Circle the verb form that best completes each sentence. If both forms are possible, circle "both."*

1. Jason Rivers _____ a crime.

   a. has committed
   b. has been committing
   c. both

2. He _____ anyone about it.

   a. hasn't told
   b. hasn't been telling
   c. both

3. Jason _____ about his crime a lot.

   a. has thought
   b. has been thinking
   c. both

4. The police _____ him once about the crime.

   a. have interviewed
   b. have been interviewing
   c. both

5. They _____ him yet.
   a. haven't arrested
   b. haven't been arresting
   c. both

TEST 2

Write several paragraphs discussing your opinion about capital punishment.

- Should people ever be executed for capital crimes? Why or why not?

- When, if ever, should capital punishment not be used?

A. *Read the excerpt.*

Why are there so many divorces in the United States? Reverend George Silver thinks there's a simple answer: It's too easy to get married. Along with other community leaders, Reverend Silver is trying to change the way people get married. He is proposing a three-month waiting period between the time a couple apply for a marriage license and when they actually get married. During that time, the couple would be required to attend marriage education classes.

"Right now, a couple can get married in only a few days, or in some states, a few hours after they first apply for a license," says Reverend Silver. "They are not required to really think about the decision they are making." As a result, many newlywed couples have not discussed important issues, such as how to raise children, manage their money, or solve problems that may occur in the marriage. However, during a divorce, Reverend Silver reminds us, couples are required to discuss the same issues: children and money. "That doesn't make sense," he says. "We should require couples to discuss these things before starting a marriage, instead of after it has failed."

1 *Circle the best answer for each question.*

1. What is the best title for the reading?
    a. "Married People Don't Talk Enough"
    b. "Marriage Is Too Easy Today"
    c. "Make Divorce More Difficult"

2. What is similar about marriage and divorce?
    a. Both are easy.
    b. Both are difficult.
    c. During both, couples deal with the same issues.

2 *What are Reverend Silver's opinions about marriage? Check (✓) the opinions he states in the reading.*

Reverend Silver thinks that _____.

_____ 1. couples should take marriage education classes before they marry

_____ 2. a marriage license isn't necessary

_____ 3. children and money are important issues

_____ 4. not enough people get divorced

B. *Complete the sentences with a word from the list.*

leadership	marriage	partnership	traditional
lifestyle	matchmaker	pregnant	unique

1. In _____ Chinese society, the goal of a marriage was to produce healthy sons.

2. The oldest son would usually take a position of _____ within the family.

3. Chinese parents often hired a _____ to help them look for the right spouse.

4. In Hopi culture, parents would let their children find their own _____ partners.

5. If a Hopi girl became _____ by her boyfriend, she would usually marry him.

6. The _____ custom called "windowing" belongs to Bavarian culture. It is seen nowhere else in the world.

7. The members of the Oneida Community in New York practiced a type of group marriage. They continued this _____ until John Noyes, their leader, left the community.

8. At first, the Mormons believed that a man could have several wives. Now they teach that marriage is a _____ between one man and one woman.

C. *Circle the word that best completes each analogy.*

1. painter : picture = matchmaker : _____
   traditional   friend   marriage

2. happy : content = permanent : _____
   similar   everlasting   romantic

3. town : mayor = group : _____
   leader   city   partner

4. parent : child = boss : _____
   tradition   employee   partner

5. make : mistakes = raise : _____
   children   produce   lifestyle

D. *Complete the sentences below with a pair of related words from the list. Change the order of the words if necessary.*

   marry/marriage
   partnership/partners
   similar/similarity
   romantic/romance
   court/courtship
   pregnancy/pregnant

1. Jennifer got _____ with her first baby a couple of months
   ago. She plans to keep working during her _____.

2. In some cultures, young men and women _____ for an
   extended period. When their _____ is over, they either
   break up or get married.

3. I think Buddy and Eva are having a secret _____. You can
   tell by the _____ way they look at each other whenever
   they're together.

4. People who _____ partners with very different backgrounds
   often have problems. In this type of _____, the spouses will
   probably have difficulty understanding each other.

5. Married people are like _____ in a business. In a business _____, both members work hard to make sure the business will be successful.

6. Doug and Erika have _____ ideas about raising children. Because of the _____ of their viewpoints, they rarely argue.

E. *Complete the following paragraph using **a(n)** or **the**.*

    When people get married they often go on _____ honeymoon.
                        1.
Honeymoons are special vacations for people who have just gotten married.
For example, _____ newlywed couple may go to _____
              2.   3.
nice hotel on their wedding night. Hotels often have special rooms called
honeymoon suites. _____ rate for _____ honeymoon suite
                       4.   5.
may include champagne and dinner for two.

TEST 2

Write several paragraphs about the importance of taking marriage education classes.

- Should people be required to take such classes before they marry? Why or why not?

Achievement Tests
Test 1 Answer Key

UNIT 1

A _____

1. 1. T   2. F   3. F
2. 1. c   2. b   3. b   4. a

B _____

1. translation
2. global
3. firm
4. message
5. goal
6. succeed
7. yell
8. competitive
9. convince
10. fail

C _____

1. all in a row
2. go over too well
3. hear of it
4. all over the place
5. take your time
6. have a hard time

D _____

1. D1   2. CS   3. D2   4. TS

E _____

1. thinks
2. isn't helping
3. is discussing
4. believes
5. is offering

UNIT 2

A _____

1. 1. F   2. T   3. F   4. F
2. 1. a   2. b   3. b   4. a

B _____

1. a
2. b
3. b
4. b
5. a
6. b
7. a
8. b
9. a
10. a

C _____

1. accomplishment
2. obsessive
3. perfect
4. gifted
5. controversial
6. intense
7. beneficial

UNIT 3 (continued)

D _____

1. can't
2. could
3. couldn't
4. been able to
5. be able to

UNIT 3

A _____

1. 1. c   2. a
2. 1. T   2. T   3. F   4. F
    5. T   6. T

B _____

1. victim
2. fraud
3. miracle
4. arthritis
5. discovery
6. clinic
7. unproven
8. offer
9. guarantee
10. qualified
11. quack
12. harmless

C _____

1. knowledgeable
2. illegal
3. untested
4. hopeless
5. misuse

D _____

1. the best
2. the most intelligent
3. the most advanced
4. the worst
5. the most famous

UNIT 4

A _____

1. 1. a   2. b
2. 1. T   2. T   3. F   4. F
    5. F

B _____

1. j
2. a
3. d
4. i
5. e
6. g
7. c
8. f
9. h
10. k
11. b
12. l

C

1. c
2. a
3. b
4. c
5. a
6. c

D

1. to wake up the children
2. to steal some money
3. to go on a trip
4. to keep it from crying
5. to lose some weight

UNIT 5

A

1 1. F   2. T   3. F

2 1. doctor   3. bachelorette
   2. poetess   4. actor

B

1. b
2. c
3. a
4. a
5. c
6. b
7. b
8. a
9. c
10. b

C

1. also
2. On the other hand
3. In contrast to
4. Unlike
5. Likewise
6. However
7. Similarly

D

a. Could I ask you a question?
b. Could you pass me the butter?
c. Let's go to my house.
d. Throw me the ball.
e. Would you mind getting the tickets?
f. This store is great, isn't it?

1. e
2. a
3. c
4. d
5. b
6. f

UNIT 6

A

1 1. b   2. a   3. a
2 1. F   2. T   3. F   4. T

B

1. remote
2. consequence
3. landscape
4. tourists
5. vast
6. preserve
7. ozone hole
8. fragile
9. continent
10. coastal
11. harsh
12. inhabited

C

1. remote
2. ice
3. harsh
4. report
5. garbage
6. floods
7. destroy

D

1. took
2. was listening
3. arrived
4. were waiting

UNIT 7

A

1 1. T   2. F   3. T
2 1. b   2. b   3. a   4. a

B

1. ambition
2. dignity
3. flirt
4. bicker
5. mean
6. stunts
7. opportunity
8. limited

C

1. loving
2. perfect
3. believable
4. henpecked
5. tension
6. charming

D

1. hard-working
2. an excellent wife
3. takes care of the family
4. prepare them to be good citizens
5. saving money

E

1. what Alex / he did last night
2. how I feel
3. where they are / they're going
4. What Sara / she wants

UNIT 8

A ———————————————

| 1 | 1. F | 2. T | 3. T | |
| 2 | 1. b | 2. a | 3. b | 4. a |

B ———————————————

1. f   5. e
2. g   6. a
3. c   7. b
4. d   8. h

C ———————————————

1. b   4. a
2. a   5. b
3. b   6. b

D ———————————————

1. As a result   4. Since
2. because   5. Consequently
3. therefore

E ———————————————

1. used to   3. used to
2. didn't use to   4. didn't use to

UNIT 9

A ———————————————

| 1 | 1. b | 2. c | 3. b | |
| 2 | 1. F | 2. T | 3. T | 4. F |

B ———————————————

FOR

1. victims   4. killer
2. fair   5. message
3. lifestyle   6. murder

AGAINST

1. cruel   4. act
2. type   5. execution
3. Innocent   6. chance

C ———————————————

1. b   4. a
2. a   5. b
3. a   6. a

D ———————————————

1. a   4. a
2. a   5. a
3. c

UNIT 10

A ———————————————

| 1 | 1. b | 2. c | | |
| 2 | 1. ✓ | 2. (blank) | 3. ✓ | 4. (blank) |

B ———————————————

1. traditional   5. pregnant
2. leadership   6. unique
3. matchmaker   7. lifestyle
4. marriage   8. partnership

C ———————————————

1. marriage   4. employee
2. everlasting   5. children
3. leader

D ———————————————

1. pregnant/pregnancy   4. marry/marriage
2. court/courtship   5. partners/partnership
3. romance/romantic   6. similar/similarity

E ———————————————

1. a   4. The
2. a   5. the
3. a

TestGen is software that helps you create your own tests from the *NorthStar* Achievement Tests.

Installing TestGen on Windows® Computers

- Insert the TestGen CD-ROM into your computer's CD-ROM drive.
- Open **My Computer**. Then double-click the CD-ROM drive, illustrated by the ⊙ symbol.
- Double-click "tgsetup.exe."
- Follow the directions on the screen to complete the installation. Once the installation is complete, the program will begin automatically.

Installing TestGen on Macintosh® Computers

- Insert the TestGen CD-ROM into your computer's CD-ROM drive.
- Double-click on "TestGen_Installer."
- Follow the directions on the screen to complete the installation. Once the installation is complete, the program will begin automatically.

How to Use TestGen

- There are three ways to create tests: 1) You can use the pre-made unit tests. Open TestGen and click File > Open Test..., and then select a test. 2) You can create tests manually. Refer to page 4 of the *Quick Guide* (Quick Guide to TestGen.pdf on the TestGen CD-ROM) for instructions. 3) You can use the TestGen Wizard. If you choose this option, the test questions will appear in random order. To retain the sequence specified in the Teacher's Manual, you will need to sort the questions. Refer to page 10 of the *Quick Guide* for instructions on using the Wizard and retaining question sequence.
- The **Quick Guide** explains how to get started and use TestGen's essential tools and features. It also includes answers to many frequently asked questions. This document is on the TestGen CD-ROM in the same location as the installation file. See the "Notes" section below for information on reading a PDF file.

Product Support

- The *User's Guide* (TG5UserGuide.pdf) provides detailed instructions about how to use all of TestGen's tools and features. Once TestGen has been installed, the *User's Guide* is also available by clicking "Help" in the TestGen menu at the top of the screen.
- The CD-ROM's *Readme* (Readme.txt) provides TestGen's system requirements and more detailed installation instructions.
- Additional TestGen resources—including Frequently Asked Questions—are accessible on the NorthStar Companion Website: http://www.longman.com/northstar/.
- For further technical assistance, call Pearson's toll-free product support line: 1-800-677-6337 (M-F, 8 a.m.-5 p.m., CST); or send an e-mail to media.support@pearsoned.com.

Notes

- To view the *Quick Guide* or *User's Guide*, Adobe® Acrobat® Reader® is required. This free software can be installed from the Internet at the following address: http://www.adobe.com/products/acrobat/main.html
- The installation instructions above are for computers that ***do not*** have TestGen installed already. If your computer already has TestGen installed, see the *User's Guide* or *Readme*.
- This CD-ROM has been confirmed to work on many computer configurations around the world. However, there may be some local operating systems that do not support TestGen.